Interior Sketches III
More Ramblings around Interior Alaska historic sites
Text and drawings by Ray Bonnell

Pingo Press - Fairbanks, Alaska

Artwork, graphics and text copyright 2023 by Ray Bonnell.

All rights reserved. No part of this publication may be reproduced, stored in a retrieved system, or transmitted in any form or by any means—electronic, mechanical, photocopying, or otherwise—without the prior written permission of the publisher.

All drawings and essays related to specific historic sites were originally published in *Sketches of Alaska,* a biweekly column appearing in the *Fairbanks Daily News-Miner*. Some of the essays have been revised and expanded since original publication.

Book design, layout and formatting done at Pingo Press. Fonts used: Licinia Aged, Gil Sans, Minion Pro

Cover illustration: Fuller Thompson's cabin at Scottie Creek, a few miles from the Canadian border. (See page 8)

Frontispiece: Drawing accompanying chapter four of V*ingt-cinq ans de solitude*, a 2016 french-language edition of John Haines book of essays, *The Stars, the Snow, the Fire - Twenty-five Years in the Alaska Wilderness.*

This book would not have been possible without the support of my wife, Betsy, who has been my companion for fifty years, and voluntarily (yes—voluntarily) edits my work and acts as an artistic consultant.

Pingo Press
127 Glacier Avenue. Fairbanks, AK 99701
info@pingopress.us

Printed in the United States of America
First Printing, April 2023
ISBN 978-1-7364236-0-8

Contents

Map 1

Introduction 2

The growth and decline of Eagle's historic churches 4
      Taylor Highway - Eagle

World War II-era telephone line still in use in Upper Tanana Valley 6
      Alaska Highway - Scottie Creek

Alaska Highway ended the isolation of Scottie Creek area 8
      Alaska Highway - Scottie Creek

Tok, Alaska – a community built for the open road 10
      Alaska Highway - Tok

BLM's YCC program enriched lives of youth from across Alaska 12
      Alaska Highway - Tanacross

Bridges were among last items completed on Alaska Highway 14
      Alaska Highway - Johnson River

Parts of the Valdez-Eagle Trail can still be walked 16
      Tok Cutoff - Eagle Creek

Richardson Highway's McCallum Creek was once a busy settlement 18
      Richardson Highway - McCallum Creek

The Reverend Bert Bingle's 600 mile-long Alaska Highway parish 20
      Richardson Highway - Delta Junction

Big Delta ARC garage saw use until World War II 22
      Richardson Highway - Big Delta

Haines Pipeline supplied military fuel needs in Eastern Interior Alaska 24
      Richardson Highway - Quartz Lake Road

The changing roadhouses of Richardson, Alaska 26
      Richardson Highway - Richardson

1928 Stearman biplane made Alaska aviation history 28
      Denali National Park and Preserve - Muldrow Glacier

The Fageol Safety Bus and the Denali Park Road 30
      Parks Highway - Mckinley Village

Superintendent's office is one of oldest buildings at Denali National Park 32
      Denali National Park and Preserve - Headquarters Site

Denali National Park warehouse changes function but still serves 34
      Denali National Park and Preserve - Headquarters Site

Contents

Ebb and flow of mining at Kantishna reflected in Eldorado Creek history..**36**
    Denali National Park and Preserve - Kantishna

Suntrana Coal Mine, near Healy, is just a memory..**38**
    Parks Highway - Healy

Mears Memorial Bridge the final link in the Alaska Railroad..**40**
    Parks Highway - Nenana

Ester studio evokes memory of painter, Rusty Heurlin..**42**
    Parks Highway - Ester

The Tolovana Tram, early Livengood's jury-rigged transport system..**44**
    Elliot Highway - Livengood

Livengood Placers and its vagabond gold dredge..**46**
    Elliot Highway - Livengood

Manley's historic schoolhouse reflects town's commitment to education..**48**
    Elliot Highway - Manley

An old Manley tractor still putters along..**50**
    Elliot Highway - Manley

LeTourneau Sno-freighter made Arctic transportation history..**52**
    Steese Highway - Fox

Hi-Yu was one of Fairbanks area's most successful hard-rock gold mines..**54**
    Steese Highway - Fairbanks Creek

Fairbanks Creek Camp was one of F.E. Co.'s final ventures in Fairbanks area..**56**
    Steese Highway - Fairbanks Creek

Old FE Company camp still an important part of Chatanika..**58**
    Steese Highway - Chatanika

The changing fortunes of Old Chatanika..**60**
    Steese Highway - Chatanika

The origins of Poker Flat Research Range..**62**
    Steese Highway - Chatanika

Clarence Berry had major impact on Interior Alaska mining..**64**
    Steese Highway - Eagle Creek

Deadwood Cemetery burials tell the history of Central area..**66**
    Circle Hot Springs Road - Cemetery Road

Deadwood Creek mining camp near Central survives as family retreat..**68**
    Circle Hot Springs Road - Deadwood Creek Road

How wireless telegraphy helped modernize Circle..**70**
    Steese Highway - Circle

Contents

North Pole Grange links area with its homesteading history *72*
    North Pole - Grange Road

Haydon cabin evokes memories of homesteading along Chena Slough *74*
    North Pole - Badger Road

KJNP radio and TV celebrates 50th year of broadcasting *76*
    North Pole - Mission Road

Ladd Field began life as cold-weather testing facility *78*
    Fort Wainwright - North Post

Ladd Field grew rapidly during World War II *80*
    Fort Wainwright - North Post

Fairbanks Aeromedical Lab – Cold War-era program designed to study the Arctic *82*
    Fort Wainwright - Neely Road

Wilbur and sons played a big role in Fairbanks history *84*
    Fairbanks - Downtown, Noble Street

Music Mart: 60 years in the same Fairbanks location *86*
    Fairbanks - Downtown, Noble Street

The Northward Building still stands out in downtown Fairbanks *88*
    Fairbanks - Downtown, 3rd Avenue

Dunkel Street cabin is one of the oldest buildings in downtown Fairbanks *90*
    Fairbanks - Downtown. Dunkel Street

Modern birch-bark canoe evokes traditional Athabascan culture *92*
    Fairbanks - Downtown, Dunkel Street

The Blooms, pioneering members of the Jewish community in Fairbanks *94*
    Fairbanks - Downtown, 5th AVenue

Lathrop Building began as home for city newspaper *96*
    Fairbanks - Downtown, 2nd Avenue

Claire Fejes' home and gallery was an artistic haven *98*
    Fairbanks - Downtown, Cushman Street

R. C. Wood, one of Fairbanks' neglected early founding fathers *100*
    Fairbanks - Downtown, 1st Avenue

Christian Science one of earliest religious groups active in Fairbanks *102*
    Fairbanks - Downtown, 1st Avenue

1915 Tanana Chiefs Conference – an early step toward Alaska Native Claims Settlement Act *104*
    Fairbanks - Downtown, 1st Avenue

Old Pan American hanger is a piece of Fairbanks' hidden history *106*
    Fairbanks - Downtown, Cowles Street

v

Contents

Methodist church, forced to close in 1916, is reborn 36 year later 108
    Fairbanks - Downtown, 2nd AVenue

'Eskimo Village' survives on Lathrop Street 110
    South Fairbanks - Lathrop Street

A-67 Exposition survives as Pioneer Park 112
    Fairbanks - Pioneer Park

P&H dragline at Pioneer Park represents early 1900s industrial innovation 114
    Fairbanks - Pioneer Park, Mining Valley

Pioneer Park's Gold Dome morphs from white elephant to air museum 116
    Fairbanks - Pioneer Park

Tall caches were once common in Alaska 118
    Fairbanks - Pioneer Park, Gold Rush Town

Harry Karstens, a.k.a. the Seventymile Kid, and his Fairbanks connection 120
    Fairbanks - Pioneer Park, Gold Rush Town

"Eva's Place" can still be found at Pioneer Park 122
    Fairbanks - Pioneer Park, Gold Rush Town

Loomis Armored Car Service had roots in Alaska Gold Rush 124
    Fairbanks - Pioneer Park, Gold Rush Town

Fairbanks Daily News-Miner traces its history back to 1903 126
    Fairbanks -North Cushman Street

St. Joseph's Hospital served Fairbanks' medical needs for over 50 years 128
    Fairbanks -North Cushman Street

Phillips Field served Fairbanks aviation community's needs for 40 years 130
    Fairbanks Railroad Industrial Area - Phillips Field Road

Wheelmen pedaled winter trails during Yukon and Alaska gold rushes 132
    Fairbanks - College Road. Fountainhead Antique Auto Museum

Government surplus helped build Alaska 134
    Fairbanks - Lemeta, Kathryn Avenue

Rasmuson Library carries on the dream of Charles Bunnell 136
    University of Alaska, Fairbanks, Tanana Loop

Interior Alaska's once numerous fishwheels dwindle in number 138
    Fairbanks - Geist Road

110-year-old building returns home to Chena 140
    Fairbanks - Chena Pump Road

Peaceful Murphy Dome was once a Cold War radar surveillance site 142
    Fairbanks - Murphy Dome Road

Contents

North Pole Grange links area with its homesteading history *72*
    North Pole - Grange Road

Haydon cabin evokes memories of homesteading along Chena Slough *74*
    North Pole - Badger Road

KJNP radio and TV celebrates 50th year of broadcasting *76*
    North Pole - Mission Road

Ladd Field began life as cold-weather testing facility *78*
    Fort Wainwright - North Post

Ladd Field grew rapidly during World War II *80*
    Fort Wainwright - North Post

Fairbanks Aeromedical Lab – Cold War-era program designed to study the Arctic *82*
    Fort Wainwright - Neely Road

Wilbur and sons played a big role in Fairbanks history *84*
    Fairbanks - Downtown, Noble Street

Music Mart: 60 years in the same Fairbanks location *86*
    Fairbanks - Downtown, Noble Street

The Northward Building still stands out in downtown Fairbanks *88*
    Fairbanks - Downtown, 3rd Avenue

Dunkel Street cabin is one of the oldest buildings in downtown Fairbanks *90*
    Fairbanks - Downtown. Dunkel Street

Modern birch-bark canoe evokes traditional Athabascan culture *92*
    Fairbanks - Downtown, Dunkel Street

The Blooms, pioneering members of the Jewish community in Fairbanks *94*
    Fairbanks - Downtown, 5th AVenue

Lathrop Building began as home for city newspaper *96*
    Fairbanks - Downtown, 2nd Avenue

Claire Fejes' home and gallery was an artistic haven *98*
    Fairbanks - Downtown, Cushman Street

R. C. Wood, one of Fairbanks' neglected early founding fathers *100*
    Fairbanks - Downtown, 1st Avenue

Christian Science one of earliest religious groups active in Fairbanks *102*
    Fairbanks - Downtown, 1st Avenue

1915 Tanana Chiefs Conference – an early step toward Alaska Native Claims Settlement Act *104*
    Fairbanks - Downtown, 1st Avenue

Old Pan American hanger is a piece of Fairbanks' hidden history *106*
    Fairbanks - Downtown, Cowles Street

Contents

Methodist church, forced to close in 1916, is reborn 36 year later 108
Fairbanks - Downtown, 2nd AVenue

'Eskimo Village' survives on Lathrop Street 110
South Fairbanks - Lathrop Street

A-67 Exposition survives as Pioneer Park 112
Fairbanks - Pioneer Park

P&H dragline at Pioneer Park represents early 1900s industrial innovation 114
Fairbanks - Pioneer Park, Mining Valley

Pioneer Park's Gold Dome morphs from white elephant to air museum 116
Fairbanks - Pioneer Park

Tall caches were once common in Alaska 118
Fairbanks - Pioneer Park, Gold Rush Town

Harry Karstens, a.k.a. the Seventymile Kid, and his Fairbanks connection 120
Fairbanks - Pioneer Park, Gold Rush Town

"Eva's Place" can still be found at Pioneer Park 122
Fairbanks - Pioneer Park, Gold Rush Town

Loomis Armored Car Service had roots in Alaska Gold Rush 124
Fairbanks - Pioneer Park, Gold Rush Town

Fairbanks Daily News-Miner traces its history back to 1903 126
Fairbanks -North Cushman Street

St. Joseph's Hospital served Fairbanks' medical needs for over 50 years 128
Fairbanks -North Cushman Street

Phillips Field served Fairbanks aviation community's needs for 40 years 130
Fairbanks Railroad Industrial Area - Phillips Field Road

Wheelmen pedaled winter trails during Yukon and Alaska gold rushes 132
Fairbanks - College Road. Fountainhead Antique Auto Museum

Government surplus helped build Alaska 134
Fairbanks - Lemeta, Kathryn Avenue

Rasmuson Library carries on the dream of Charles Bunnell 136
University of Alaska, Fairbanks, Tanana Loop

Interior Alaska's once numerous fishwheels dwindle in number 138
Fairbanks - Geist Road

110-year-old building returns home to Chena 140
Fairbanks - Chena Pump Road

Peaceful Murphy Dome was once a Cold War radar surveillance site 142
Fairbanks - Murphy Dome Road

Introduction

Cabin across from Brushkana Creek Campground along the Denali Highway in 2013. A 1971 U.S.G.S. map shows it about 50 feet from the creek. The cabin was still there in 2018 – a room with a view.

Introduction

Welcome to the third installment of *Interior Sketches, Ramblings around Interior Alaska historic sites*. Over the course of 12 years and three books, I have published entries for almost 200 sites, vehicles and events that reflect the history of the region.

Hopefully, through my column in the *Fairbanks Daily News-Miner* and my books, I have helped preserve some of the history of Interior Alaska – and shed light on a few little-known, and sometimes almost-forgotten sites.

My goal when I started doing the column was to record "snapshots in time," of the region's historic sites, since, as I wrote in my first book, "many are fading away—the result of development, vandalism, accidents and time."

Unfortunately, those words are just as true today as they were then. Our historic sites continue to slip away, victims of the many dangers Alaska presents. Here are a few of the enemies of our historic sites that probably cannot be avoided:

- Accidental structure fires.
- Arson, looting and vandalism.
- Changes in terrestrial water dynamics such as deviations in the course of water channels, seasonal flooding, ice damming and localized glaciation, and rising water levels.
- Governments and individuals who fail to see the value in preserving historic structures.
- Melting permafrost.
- Old age and structural deficiencies.
- Wildfires.
- Wind- and atmospheric-water-caused damage such as roof collapse from snow load; rain and snow-caused decay; erosion caused by wind, snow and rain; and damage caused by persistent or heavy winds.

Perhaps the biggest enemy of our historic sites is apathy – of individuals and communities not caring enough about whether historic and culturally-important sites are preserved. We need to build pathways to facilitate future generations actually becoming involved in historic preservation and restoration.

Believing in the importance of preserving historic sites is not enough. And recognizing historic sites through inclusion on the National Register of Historic Places or by other means is only a starting point, and does little to actually protect historic sites.

Actions to physically protect our historic resources are required. Unfortunately, not every historic site can be preserved, but there is hope for at least some of our sites. There are many structures in the region that have been saved from ruin by individuals, organizations and governments – often acting in concert. These are sites that are being rehabilitated, or at least being stabilized and protected from imminent threats.

A case in point is the SS Nenana, located at Pioneer park in Fairbanks. It the last wooden-hulled sternwheeler to ply the waters of Alaska, and is on the National Register of Historic Places, as well being a National Historic Landmark (denoting national historic significance).

The SS Nenana, deteriorated due to years of neglect, has been on Preservation Alaska's list of Most Endangered Historic Properties in Alaska for the past five years, and just a few years ago was in danger of being torn down,

However, the community rallied to save it. A nonprofit organization, "Friends of SS Nenana," was formed (with North Star Community Foundation as its fiscal sponsor). The group's efforts prompted the boat's listing on the "Most Endangered " list, and it is working with the Fairbanks North Star Borough (which owns the boat), to renovate and preserve the steamer. The sternwheeler's future is not assured, but progress is being made.

I hope you enjoy this armchair tour of Eastern Interior Alaska historic sites (or use your *Interior Sketches* guide book to visit the sites). But I also hope you become invested in trying to preserve these sites for future travelers to visit and/or help preserve.

Taylor Highway - Eagle

St. Paul's Church in Eagle

The growth and decline of Eagle's historic churches

The first Christian missionaries in Eastern Interior Alaska did not follow the miners who began arriving toward the end of the 1800s. Rather, missionaries preceded the miners, following instead Hudson's Bay Company as it set up trading posts. Thus, Anglican missionaries established a mission at Fort Yukon in 1862 to serve Athabascan Indians, and then began reaching out to surrounding villages along the Yukon River.

One of those villages was located just upriver from present-day Eagle. French-Canadian fur trader Francois

Mercier opened a trading post he called Belle Isle near the village in 1874, and later moved the trading post downriver a few miles to a creek the Athabascans called Tototlindu.

According to Melody Webb's book, *Yukon, the Last Frontier*, the Rev. Vincent Sim started a mission adjacent to the trading post in the early 1880s — hence the change in the watercourse's name to "Mission Creek."

Unfortunately, Rev. Sim, who was an itinerant priest, died in 1885 at Old Rampart, an Athabascan village along the Porcupine River where a Hudson's Bay trading post and an Anglican mission were located. The fledgling church at Mission Creek subsequently fell into disuse.

It was not until after the city of Eagle was established in 1898 that organized religion returned. The first churchman to set up shop was Father Francis Monroe, a Jesuit priest. He stepped off a boat on Aug. 10, 1899.

A Catholic family leaving town sold him a lot with two cabins, and the larger cabin became the chapel of St. Francis Xavier.

A month later Presbyterians arrived. The Rev. James Kirk and his wife, Anna, moved into a small cabin and for a time held services in a saloon.

The Kirks came with only the "essentials," including china, linens and other household goods — even a sewing machine and washing machine. A history of the Presbyterian Church in Alaska relates that they also brought along a piano for their future church. Unfortunately, the piano was too large to fit through their cabin door, and for a time sat crated on the cabin's front porch.

The Kirks eventually built a log church with attached residence overlooking the Yukon River at the end of Chamberlain Street. As with many churches in frontier Alaska, they set up a reading room in a corner of their residence to entice men out of the local saloons.

Unfortunately for Eagle, the Klondike gold rush soon petered out. When gold was discovered at Nome in 1900, most able-bodied men abandoned Eagle, and its population plummeted to about 100. Then, in 1902 gold was discovered in the hills above the Chena River, Fairbanks bloomed, and Eagle's population shrank further.

Father Monroe struggled on a few more years in Eagle, but in 1904 shuttered St. Francis Xavier Chapel and moved to Fairbanks to establish a new church.

In 1902, the Episcopal Church, carrying on the work of the Anglican Church along the Yukon River, established a church in Eagle Village, the Athabascan community a few miles north of the white community. (When Hudson's Bay Company vacated Fort Yukon after the U.S. purchase of Alaska, the Canadian Anglican Church also relinquished its missions to its kindred U.S. Episcopalians.)

The Presbyterian Church, due to declining membership, transferred its property in Eagle to the Episcopal Church in 1905. The Eagle Village church became St. John's, and the church in Eagle became St. Paul's.

Declining attendance eventually forced the closure of St. Paul's and the church property was transferred to the Eagle Historical Society. The drawing is of St. Paul's Church in the 1990s after the adjacent residence was torn down. The building is still used for weddings and other special occasions.

Sources:

- *A Century of Faith, Episcopal Diocese of Alaska*, 1895-1995. Centennial Press. 1995
- "History, Presbytery of the Yukon, 1899-1988." Jessie DeVries. Yukon Presbytery website. 2007
- Photo of St. Paul's Church – c. 1913. Walter and Lillian Phillips Photograph Collection. UAF Archives
- Photos of St. Paul's Church. Historic American Building Survey, National Park Service. 1984
- "The Alaskan Missions of the Episcopal Church, A brief sketch, historical and descriptive." Hudson Stuck. Domestic and Foreign Missionary Society, 1920
- *Yukon, the Last Frontier*, Melody Webb. University of Nebraska Press. 1985

A portion of the Alaska Military Telephone Line along the Alaska Highway near the Canadian border

World War II-era telephone line still in use in Upper Tanana Valley

The Alaska Highway, built in 1942, was not the only World War II-era construction project linking Alaska with the rest of North America. The Alaska Military Telephone Line (AMTL), stretching 2,020 miles from Edmonton, Alberta, to Fairbanks was also built during that period.

According to the Center of Military History's book, *U.S. Army In World War II; The Signal Corps, The Test*, three communications technologies were incorporated into the project: radio, telephone and teletype. Radio, the most portable, followed Alaska Highway construction crews into the field. However, because of atmospheric and magnetic interference at higher latitudes, radio was not always reliable. Consequently, a telephone and teletype line paralleling the highway was also planned.

Because of wartime demands, U.S. Army Signal Corps personnel were needed elsewhere and could not be spared for the project. Private contractors built much of the line.

The line was approved for construction in June 1942. However, planning consumed the next five months and work did not start until November.

The first section of AMTL, from Edmonton to Dawson Creek, British Columbia, was perhaps the most difficult to build. Frigid winter conditions meant workers had to bore holes in frozen soil to install poles. Crews were also missing crucial supplies. For instance, 400 miles of poles were installed before crews received crossbars on which to attach the wire.

There were also unanticipated design changes. During World War II copper was designated a strategic raw material, and the War Production Board disapproved the use of all-copper wire for the AMTL, substituting copper-clad steel wire instead. The substituted wire did not provide the same long-distance transmission characteristics, so additional repeater stations were needed.

Myriad other problems delayed construction, including lumber shortages, freak weather conditions, and lack of worker housing. To meet a Dec. 1 deadline for getting the first section operational, only a skeletal system was installed.

The schedule called for completing the next section, as far as Whitehorse, Yukon Territory by May 1. Winter weather, and correcting deficiencies in the original line slowed line-work considerably, though. By the end of January 1943, it became evident that the only way to ensure the project's timely completion was to bring in Signal Corps troops. On March 1, the 255th Signal Construction Company left San Francisco. Corps of Engineer troops were temporarily pressed into service until the Signal Corp troops arrived.

The second section was completed three weeks later than anticipated, on May 22. On that day a call was placed over the line from Whitehorse to Washington D.C..

In the early summer of 1943 work started on the final section. Favorable weather meant work progressed rapidly. There was one 50-mile stretch of particularly bad road just east of the Canada border, however.

Corps of Engineer crews had punched through that road section during the previous winter when the ground was frozen. Troops had simply scraped off the insulating muskeg and graded the underlying frozen ground. When the ground thawed in the spring the road became a seemingly bottomless bog. It took a 20-man Signal Corps detachment, supplied by horseback, four weeks to put in that section of line.

By the middle of October 1943 the line was completed. Ken Coates book, *North to Alaska*, mentions that 95,000 poles and 14,000 miles of wire were used in the project.

Sections of the World War II-era line, some with poles tilting at crazy angles, can still be seen along the Alaska Highway in the Upper Tanana River Valley. Portions of the line are still used for local telephone service.

Sources:

- *Getting the Message Through, A Branch History of the U.S. Army Signal Corps.* Rebecca Raines. Center of Military History. 2011
- *North to Alaska, Fifty Years of the World's Most Remarkable Highway.* Ken Coates. University of Alaska Press. 1992
- *U.S. Army in World War II: The Signal Corps: The Test.* George Thompson et al. Center of Military History. 2003

Fuller Thompson cabin at Scottie Creek in 2019. Thompson was a big-game guide and he and his wife were among the first homesteaders in the Scottie Creek area.

Alaska Highway ended the isolation of Scottie Creek area

Scottie Creek crosses the Alaska Highway 2.5 miles from the Alaska-Canada border, about a mile west of the U.S. Customs station. Just west of the Scottie Creek bridge, on the south side of the highway, there once stood a small cluster of abandoned structures. Those moldering buildings were all that was left of Thompson's Borderline Camp, a business operated in the 1960s and 70s by Fuller and Dorothy Thompson, early homesteaders in the area.

Scottie Creek is located at the eastern-most upstream limit of the Tanana Valley. Named for a member of an 1898 U.S.G.S. survey party, the stream originates in Alaska but loops through Canada, flowing 50 miles before emptying into the Chisana River—a tributary of the Tanana River.

Long before Westerners entered the region, the valley was home to the Scottie Creek band of Upper Tanana Athabascan Indians. Prior to the 19th century these Athabascans practiced a semi-nomadic lifestyle based on seasonal exploitation of the area's natural resources. They obtained trade goods from coastal Chilkat Tlingit.

Not until the mid 1880s, and the discovery of gold along the Fortymile River (about 100 miles to the north), did Westerners begin filtering into the area. After western contact many Upper Tanana Athabascans trekked as far as Tanana, Eagle and Fortymile to trade for western goods.

The short-lived 1913-14 gold rush at Chisana, about 50 miles southwest of Scottie Creek, brought more Westerners. However, the area still remained extremely isolated, and non-Native residents were limited to big-game hunters, trappers and traders.

Construction of the Alaska Highway in 1942 finally ended Scottie Creek's isolation. A 2015 U.S. Fish and Wildlife Service report states that one of the area's residents at that time was Fuller Seth Thompson, a big-game guide. Fuller assisted with surveying and construction of the highway, and remained in the area after World War II. During the 1950s he homesteaded at Scottie Creek, building a cabin on the west bank of the creek several hundred yards south of the highway.

His cabin (shown in the drawing) faces southeast towards Scottie Creek and is located on high ground between the creek and several small lakes to the north. The cabin is 12' wide by 16' long, with a low-pitched metal-covered gable roof. It is constructed of unpeeled logs saddle-notched at the corners.

The interior side walls are only about 4 1/2' high, with the ceiling about 7' high at the ridge-pole. The front door is less than 5' high and is flanked by small windows. The front windows have wood shelves beneath them. The southwest, northwest and northeast walls each have a single window. Much of the sod chinking between the logs is intact, and the cabin is still in good condition.

Other structures at the site include a collapsed metal shed, another collapsed structure that might have been a meat-drying rack, a cache, outhouse, and two log doghouses.

In 1968 the Thompsons applied for a trade and manufacturing site next to the highway, and about that time they opened "Thompson's Borderline Camp." According to 1971 and 1972 issues of *The Milepost* and other sources, the Thompsons operated a duty-free liquor store, post office, gift shop, and garage, and rented out "unmodern" cabins.

Fuller died unexpectedly in 1972 and was buried adjacent to his cabin. Dorothy evidently operated the business after his death, and according to *The Milepost* the post office was open at least until 1979. When Dorothy died in 1993 her ashes were spread on Fuller's grave.

When I visited the site in 2019 only five buildings were left from the business. All were dilapidated and the site contaminated. The property is now part of Tetlin National Wildlife Refuge, and the National Wildlife Service recently demolished the buildings.

Based on the age and apparent historical significance of Thompson's cabin, the U.S. Fish and Wildlife Service hopes to rehabilitate it and related structures for use as an interpretive site about Scottie Creek history.

Sources:

- Conversations with Shawn Bayless, refuge manager for Tetlin National Wildlife Refuge.
- "2015 Report of Cultural Resources Located at Milepost 1223 of the Alaska Highway within the Tetlin National Wildlife Refuge." Robert Meinhardt, Amy Ramiriz & Kyle Beargeon. U.S. Fish and Wildlife Service. 2015
- Listings for Scottie Creek in 1971, 1972 and 1979 issues of *The Milepost: All-the-North Travel Guide*. "Navigability Report, Upper Chisana and Ladue River Drainage Areas." U.S. Bureau of Land Management. 1983
- "Wild Resource Use in Northway, Alaska." Martha F. Case. Alaska Department of Fish and Game. 1986

1962 Kenworth truck with Holmes model 750 25-ton wrecker seen in Tok in 2011

Tok, Alaska – a community built for the open road

Tok, with 1300 residents, is the largest community in the Upper Tanana Valley in Eastern Interior Alaska.

Before construction of the Alcan Highway in the 1940s, most Westerners were interlopers in the Upper Tanana River area. Athabascan Indians have lived in the area for generations. At the beginning of the nineteenth century a string of villages, including Healy Lake, Mansfield Lake, Tetlin, Old Tetlin, and Nabesna (Northway) were located along the hundred-mile section of the Tanana River nearest the Canadian border.

The Valdez-Eagle Trail (1899-1901) and Washington-Alaska Military Cable and Telegraph System (1900-

1904) were built through the area, and the Episcopal Church established a mission at Tanacross (just south of Mansfield Lake) in 1912. A few traders, such as John Hajdukovich, opened stores at some Native villages. Gold discoveries to the north along tributaries of the 40-Mile River, and along rivers such as the Chisana and Chistochina to the south lured prospectors. For the most part, though, people headed for the diggings only passed through the area.

The situation changed dramatically with construction of the Alcan Highway in 1942, and the routing of the highway's Alaska section down the Tanana Valley.

The U.S. government was eager to punch through the 1500-mile-long Alcan in one building season, so construction began in the spring of 1942 at numerous points along the proposed route. Janet Haigh, in her book, *The Alaska Highway, a Historic Photographic Journey,* points out that responsibility for the segment from Alaska into Canada fell to the U.S. Army's 97th Engineering Regiment, an all-black unit.

When the 97th landed at Valdez in April of 1942 its first task was just reaching the remote Tanana Valley location where it would begin work on the Alcan. The shortest route for a new road from Valdez to the Tanana and the U.S./Canadian border started at Slana, 63 road-miles northwest of the Richardson Highway's Gakona Junction. From Slana north over Mentasta Pass to the Tanana River was about 70 miles.

Soldiers from the 97th widened and improved sections of the Richardson Highway and Gulkana-Slana Road as they worked northward. Finally, in early July, they began cutting a new road through the wilds northwest of Slana, roughly following the path of the almost abandoned Valdez-Eagle Trail.

By mid-August the lead party reached a point just south of the Tanana River, a few miles from its confluence with the Tok River. It was there that the yet-to-be constructed Alcan Highway would intersect with the newly-blazed Slana Cutoff (now called the Tok Cutoff).

According to Donna Blasor-Bernhardt's book, *Tok, The Real Story*, the 97th established a tent camp and supply depot at the intersection, took a right turn, and started blazing a road towards the Canadian border. A civilian contractor, Lytle and Green, built the 100-mile section of highway between Delta Junction and Tok while the 97th worked its way east.

In the summer of 1943 the Northern Commercial Company built a store at Tok and the camp began morphing from temporary worker housing to permanent community. A townsite was laid out in 1946, which was also the year that the highway opened to civilian traffic. In 1947, a school was built at Tok and the U.S. Customs established a station there. The Customs station moved to the border 80 miles away in the 1970s, but Tok has remained an important service, supply and transportation center for Eastern Interior Alaska.

Because of the community's history as a transportation center, I thought the old wrecker pictured in the drawing would be an appropriate subject. It is a 1962 Kenworth truck with a Holmes model 750 25-ton wrecker unit. Owned by Willard Grammont of Willard's Auto in Tok, it has been cruising Eastern Interior Alaska highways for decades assisting stranded motorists.

Sources:

- Conversation with Willard Grammont, long-time Tok resident
- *The Alaska Highway, A Historic Photographic Journey*. Janet Haigh. Wolf Creek Books. 2001
- *The Upper Tanana Indians*. Robert A. McKennan. Yale University. 1959
- "Tok Community Profile." Alaska State Department of Commerce, Community and Economic Development. 2016
- *Tok: The Real Story*. Donna Blazor-Bernhardt. Winter Cabin Productions. 1996

Alaska Highway - Tanacross

Tanacross YCC camp wellhouse in 2012

BLM's YCC program enriched lives of youth from across Alaska

The small log cabin depicted in the drawing is the last vestige of the Bureau of Land Management's Youth Conservation Corps (YCC) camp at Tanacross, which is located near Tok. The building is the camp's wellhouse, constructed in the early 1970s.

The YCC, patterned after the Civilian Conservation Corps of the 1930s, is a federally-funded summer program, which in its early years, was administered in Alaska by the U.S. Forest Service, Bureau of Land Management (BLM), National Park Service, and the Alaska Department of Natural Resources. Its purpose is to provide summer work opportunities for young people (ages 15-18) and expose them to our country's natural and cultural resources.

The program was authorized by Congress in 1970. BLM began a YCC program in Interior Alaska in about 1974.

According to a 1977 Fairbanks Daily News-Miner article, the first Interior Alaska YCC camp was at 60-mile Steese Highway (Cripple Creek campground), but in 1977 the camp moved to the World War II-era Tanacross military airfield site, which was transferred to BLM after the war. (The Big Dipper ice arena here in Fairbanks is the former hanger from the Tanacross airfield.)

The YCC operated out of tents at the Tanacross Camp through the 1970s. A 1976 BLM report of YCC projects in Eastern Interior Alaska contains a sketch map of the site showing half a dozen tent sites, plus the wellhouse, sanitation facilities, and a kitchen area.

Kirk Hoessle, who worked with BLM's YCC program from 1976 to 1980, told me that all the camp facilities were tents except for the kitchen facility (which was an ATCO unit), and the log wellhouse. Kirk said that the camp was used for training and team-building, and for rest-and-relaxation between projects. Otherwise the 10-person teams were out in the field, either involved with construction or maintenance projects (such as building the Wickersham Creek trail shelter in the White Mountains) or participating in resource inventory activities.

When I visited the Tanacross site in 2012 the tent platforms were gone, replaced by 8' by 16' wood-frame plywood-sheathed buildings on post-and-pad foundations.

The wood buildings weren't used for long, though. The YCC program lost Congressional funding in 1980. (Some states, seeing the benefit of YCC activities, continued it at the state level, and, beginning in 1992, the YCC and similar programs have seen a resurgence at the private, state and federal level. At the federal level, the YCC limped along after 1980 with agencies providing funds from their operating budgets. At some point during the 1980s BLM ended its Interior Alaska YCC program, mothballing the Tanacross camp. When I visited, the metal-roofed wood-frame buildings were still in good condition, but the sod-roofed wellhouse showed a definite lack of maintenance. If you look closely at the drawing, those are trees growing out of the wellhouse roof.

All the YCC camp buildings except for the wellhouse are gone now. After a windstorm in the fall of 2012 wreaked havoc in the Tanacross and Tok area, the YCC camp was cleaned up, and the wood-frame buildings, which were undamaged, were moved to the nearby Tanacross Native village.

Now, except for the wellhouse and a few isolated pipes and other debris poking through the forest duff, nothing is left of the camp—save for a small stand of lodgepole pine. Colin Cogley, a current BLM recreation specialist, told me that near where the camp used to be is a small stand of the trees. Lodgepole pines are not native to Alaska. Perhaps a YCC crew planted a few pines as a team-building experience, and those trees thrived—testament to a neglected but important part of Interior Alaska history.

Sources:

- "BLM Projects for the Fortymile Resource Area." Meredith Lockwood & James Bell. Bureau of Land Management. 1976
- Conversation with Kirk Hoessle, former BLM employee who worked with YCC program
- Conversation with Colin Cogley, BLM recreation specialist
- "The Modern Corps Movement." From "CCC Legacy," on the *Civilian Conservation Corps Legacy* website, <ccclegacy.org>
- "Youths at Work and Play." In *Fairbanks Daily News-Miner*. 6-18-1997

Alaska Highway - Johnson River

The Johnson River Bridge, at Mile 1380 of the Alaska Highway, was constructed in 1944

Bridges were among last items completed on Alaska Highway

The dedication of the Alaska Highway on Nov. 20, 1942, received great publicity. However, stories often paid scant attention to the actual condition of the road when it first began accepting through traffic. The public could be forgiven for thinking that the highway was finished to civilian standards, essentially ready for any traffic the U.S. military and civilian population could send over it.

Janet Haigh's book, *The Alaska highway: A Historic Photographic Journey*, relates that by the end of 1942 the Alaska Highway was actually little more than a rough track wandering through the wilderness. The road was narrow and often winding, with corduroyed sections (road bed with gravel-covered wood poles laid across it) through marshy areas, and overly steep grades in other places.

Wooden culverts and simple timber-bridges forded small creeks. Larger piling- or timber-trestle bridges, as well as pontoon bridges and ferries, were used to cross bigger streams and rivers.

The road was only passable by vehicles with high ground clearance and preferably 4- or 6-wheel drive. In the summer, vehicles had to navigate muddy roads that were prone to washout. Winter brought its own problems, with mechanical problems caused by sub-zero temperatures, and road sections that repeatedly flooded with overflow and became encased in multiple layers of ice.

According to K.S. Coats and W.R. Morrison's book, *The Alaska Highway in World War II: The U.S. Army of occupation in Canada's Northwest*, when Canada and the United States signed the agreement allowing the U.S. to build the highway across Canadian territory, the initial goal was to build a road "to a standard sufficient only for the supply of troops engaged in the work." The road was built to minimum military standards, and military convoys were the primary users — capable of navigating the rough road, and able to rescue anyone who had trouble along the way.

The agreement further stipulated that the highway would be completed to civilian highway standards by 1943. This included widening the road, installing concrete culverts, and replacing most of the wooden bridges with steel ones.

The U.S. Public Roads Administration (PRA), which had toiled alongside the U.S. military to construct the initial road, assumed responsibility for its completion after November 1942. The PRA faced a monumental task. The spring thaw in 1943 undid much of the work accomplished the previous year.

With no experience in building roads in permafrost areas, insulating vegetation was often scraped from the ground during initial roadbed construction. This exposed the permafrost to thawing and resulted in sections of road that turned to quagmires the next summer. The PRA and its civilian contractors ended up rebuilding most of the highway.

Civilian engineers also determined that much of the route punched through by the military was unsatisfactory. Eventually, 67 percent of the road was rerouted, sometimes up to 10 miles away from the original route. By the end of 1943 the PRA had completed most of its highway improvements, except for bridge replacement.

To speed bridge construction, the PRA used standardized designs wherever possible. Warren trusses (named for James Warren, who, along with Willoughby Monzani, patented the truss in 1848) were used in many of the bridges. Bridge components were fabricated in the Lower 48 states and then shipped north.

The PRA used Warren trusses 200' long and 24.5' wide. Short bridges used a single truss. For longer bridges additional trusses were added. One of the longest World War II era bridges along the Alaska Highway is the Gerstle River Bridge just south of Delta Junction, which has nine segments.

The bridge shown in the drawing is the Johnson River Bridge, at Mile 1380 of the Alaska Highway, 66 miles northwest of Tok. Composed of five Warren trusses, it's length is listed at 970.2 feet.

The Johnson River Bridge, along with most of the PRA's steel bridge replacements, was completed by 1944. Only a handful these World War II era bridges remain along the entire Alaska Highway, four of them in Alaska. As the Alaska highway is slowly improved to accommodate modern vehicles and traffic, even these bridges will probably eventually disappear.

Sources:

- *The Alaska highway: A Historic Photographic Journey.* Janet Haigh. Wolf Creek books. 2001
- *The Alaska Highway in World War II: The U.S. Army of occupation in Canada's Northwest.* K.S Coates & W. R Morrison. University of Oklahoma Press. 1992.

Segment of Valdez-Eagle Trail at Eagle Trail State Recreation Site in Fall 2016

Parts of the Valdez-Eagle Trail can still be walked

In the wake of the first wave of stampeders to the Klondike Gold Rush, U.S. Army Captain P.H. Ray was sent to Alaska in 1897 to investigate rumors of unrest among gold-seekers along the U.S. portion of the Yukon River. During his travels, Ray heard from prospectors clamoring for an "All-American" route to the Yukon gold fields that would bypass the Canadian-controlled White Pass and Chilkoot Trails.

Ray recommended that a military trail be built from the ice-free port of Valdez on Prince William Sound to the Yukon River Basin. In the summer of 1898 U.S. Army Captain William Abercrombie came to Alaska to assess the situation and reconnoiter the best route from tidewater to the Copper Basin

Abercrombie discovered horrendous conditions at Valdez. Unscrupulous promoters had convinced 4,000+ Yukon gold-seekers to attempt a trail out of Valdez. However, the trail they promoted took travelers across the Valdez and Klutina glaciers and down the tumultuous Klutina River.

Ken Marsh, in his book, *The Trail, the story of the historic Valdez-Fairbanks Trail*, estimates that only a quarter of those who attempted the Valdez Glacier trail made it as far as the Copper River, and only a handful pressed on to the Klondike. Numerous gold-seekers lost their lives on the treacherous glacier crossing, and Abercrombie estimated that 95% of those who survived the glacier trek wrecked their boats descending the Klutina River. Of those who gave up and returned to Valdez, most ended up destitute.

Captain Abercrombie returned to Washington, D.C. later that year to present his report. In 1899 he traveled back to Valdez to begin construction of a "Trans-Alaska Military Road" from Valdez to Eagle (via a glacier-free route through Keystone Canyon and across Thompson Pass). Abercrombie hired many of the destitute argonauts as construction workers

Workers built 93 miles of packhorse trail, and blazed another 112 miles of foot trail that year. The military road, also referred to as the Valdez-Eagle Trail, was completed by 1901.

Following Native trails for much of its length, the 425-mile-long trail crossed the Chugach Mountains, then followed the Copper River north and northeast before crossing the Mentasta Mountains.

Coming out of the mountains near the Tanana River, the trail swung northwest, crossing the Tanana near present-day Tanacross and going on to the Athabascan village at Lake Mansfield. Thence it climbed northeast through another Athabascan village called Ketchunstuck and into the Fortymile River region before tacking to the east through the gold camp of Franklin and then north to Eagle.

The Trans-Alaska Military Road was never more than a packhorse trail, and its years of service were few. By the time the trail was completed the Klondike Gold Rush was winding down.

Then, the discovery of gold in the Tanana Valley diverted attention away from Eagle. Starting in about 1903 gold-seekers began peeling off from the Valdez-Eagle Trail at Gakona, headed for Fairbanks. The lower half of the trail became part of the Valdez-Fairbanks Trail, while travel along the northern half declined.

During the trail's early years, the Washington-Alaska Military Cable and Telegraph System (WAMCATS) constructed telegraph lines between Valdez and Eagle, with telegraph stations located approximately every 40 miles. A Bureau of Land Management brochure states that soldiers operating and maintaining the telegraph system frequently used the trail, but even that usage began disappearing in 1909 as WAMCATS gradually converted to wireless telegraphy.

There was active mining in the Fortymile region so the trail between there and Eagle remained well-traveled. However, subsistence activities and other localized travel became predominant along most of the Valdez-Eagle Trail north of Gakona. It would take later mineral development and transportation needs to resurrect other portions of the trail.

The section of trail shown in the drawing, located 16 miles south of Tok at Eagle Trail State Recreation Site, is one of the few easily accessible segments of the original trail. Winding along the base of the mountains, it has been incorporated into a short nature trail through the recreation site.

Sources:

- "History of the Valdez Trail." Geoffrey Bleakley. Wrangell-St. Elias National Park and Preserve website. No date
- "The Eagle-Valdez Trail, Northern Portion." U.S. Bureau of Land Management. No date
- *The Trail: the story of the historic Valdez-Fairbanks Trail that opened Alaska's vast Interior*. Kenneth Marsh. Trapper Creek Museum. 2008
- Signage at Eagle Trail State Recreation Site..

McCallum Creek telegraph station ruins in 2019

Richardson Highway's McCallum Creek was once a busy settlement

McCallum Creek is a tributary of Phelan Creek, which in turn flows into the Delta River. (Several early guidebooks confused Phelan Creek with the Delta River.)

Located about 160 miles southeast of Fairbanks along what used to be the Valdez-Fairbanks Trail (now the Richardson Highway), in the early 1900s the area hosted both a busy roadhouse and a Washington-Alaska Cable and Telegraph System (WAMCATS) telegraph station.

Mail carriers and goldseekers blazed a winter trail from Gakona to Fairbanks soon after gold was discovered in the Tanana Valley in 1902. The Alaska Road Commission (ARC) began improving that trail in 1905. In the summer of 1905 a Mrs. McCallum began operating a roadhouse out of a small single-story log cabin on the east bank of Phelan Creek, just downstream from McCallum Creek.

The winter-only trail ran down the frozen Phelan Creek, and McCallum's Roadhouse was on a small point jutting into the creek bed. Under calm conditions it was easily visible to trail users. At night a large lantern hung outside the door to welcome travelers.

However, Phelan Creek was situated along one of the most treacherous sections of the Valdez-Fairbanks Trail. It was just north of Isabel pass, and deep snows were normal during winter.

The creek was also prone to overflow, making travel difficult. In addition, the narrow valley funneled wind from the Gulkana Glacier, often pushing blizzards before it. Ken Marsh, in his book, *The Trail: The Story of the Historic Valdez-Fairbanks Trail*, writes that the roadhouse, built near the exposed creek bed, was sometimes buried by snow drifts with only its stovepipe showing.

Charlie Yost took over the roadhouse in the winter of 1906-07. He built a two-story log building next to the old structure. Even it was often buried to its eaves by snow.

Yost operated the roadhouse for several years, and after he moved on it continued to be called Yost's. Turnover of roadhouse operators was rapid throughout its short existence.

The winter of 1912-13 was severe, and 12 people died along Phelan Creek trying to find Yost's. To rectify this problem the Army Signal Corps stretched a fence made of several strands of wire across the creek. Travelers lost in a blizzard would be stopped by the fence before blundering past the roadhouse. Aided by the sound of a 150-pound bell atop a post near the roadhouse that would ring in the wind, travelers could follow the fence and the sound of the bell to safety.

Yost's Roadhouse only lasted until the mid 1910s. Severe flooding forced the abandonment of the roadhouse in 1916, although the buildings continued to be used seasonally by hunters. The roadhouse was in an exposed area, and according to Walter Phillips' book, *Roadhouses of the Richardson Highway*, nothing remains of it.

However, 3/10 mile upstream are the remains of McCallum telegraph station. About a 1/4 mile northwest of the McCallum Creek Bridge on the Richardson Highway, the telegraph station ruins lie on a bypassed curve of the highway

The station was established in 1907 by the Army signal Corps, and consisted of a two-story log telegraph office/residence, a barn, large cache, and several smaller structures. Made redundant by wireless telegraphy (radio) in 1925, the station closed. The facilities were then transferred to the ARC before eventually being abandoned.

The only surviving structure is the barn, shown in the drawing. The approximately 10-foot by 20-foot metal-roofed log barn was converted into a garage, probably by the ARC, before falling into disuse. Except for a few tires and scraps of metal scattered along the old section of road, the building, which is slowly collapsing into the willows, is the last vestige of a once busy settlement.

Sources:

- *Roadhouses of the Richardson Highway, the first quarter century, 1898 to 1923*. Walter Phillips. Alaska Historical Commission. 1984
- *Roadhouses of the Richardson Highway II*. Walter Phillips. Alaska Historical Commission. 1985
- *The Trail, the Story of the Historic Valdez-Fairbanks Trail*. Kenneth Marsh. Trapper Creek Museum. 2008.

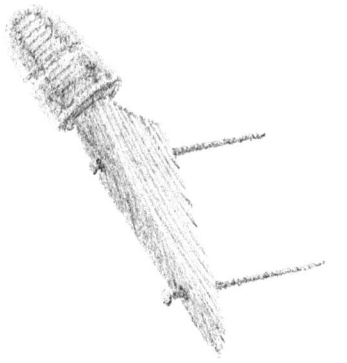

Old Presbyterian chapel at Delta Junction, built in 1952. It was one of three chapels built to support the highway parish

The Reverend Bert Bingle's 600 mile-long Alaska Highway parish

Bert Bingle was a Presbyterian minister who came to Cordova in 1928 to serve the people along the Copper River and Northwestern Railroad, and then moved to Palmer in 1935 to start a church at the Matanuska Colony. In 1941 he was assigned to a railroad ministry along the Alaska Railroad as well as ministering to scattered settlements along the Glenn and Richardson Highways.

On one of his trips along the Richardson Highway, Bert noticed Army personnel setting up camp near the new Civil Aeronautics Administration airfield near Big Delta (now referred to as Delta Junction). Finding that the new unit had no chaplain, he volunteered and served as a chaplain at the airfield (now Fort Greely) for 4 1/2 years until a military chaplain replaced him.

Discovering that construction was beginning on the 1,500 mile-long Alaska Highway, he also offered to assist the few chaplains serving along the construction route between Delta Junction and Whitehorse.

In a 1965 interview, Bert states that he and his compatriot chaplains also on several occasions went part way up the Canol Road, which ran 620 miles northwest from the Whitehorse area to Norman Wells in Northwest Territories. The Canol Road serviced the Canol Pipeline, a World War II-era oil pipeline that originated at Norman Wells.

One of the units that he assisted with was the 97th Engineers — an all black unit. In Bert's self-published book about his years in Alaska he wrote that the men of the 97th worked under harsh conditions, living in tents year-round.

He wrote that food and clothing were scarce. At times soldiers had to borrow clothes from other men, and send those who loaned them to bed so the soldiers could go out and do needed work. He also reported that on one occasion he worshipped with the 87th in an unheated building with the temperature inside hovering around 15 degrees below zero.

He and Reverend David Crawford, another Presbyterian minister who joined his highway ministry in 1943, used their own vehicles to drive the rough pioneer road. When their cars became stuck or refused to run, they hitchhiked, stopping at road construction and maintenance camps, telephone repeater stations, military airfields and the few Athabascan villages located near the road right-of-way.

After the war ended and the Alaska Highway opened to civilian traffic, Bert continued his ministry along the road, which became known as the Highway Parish. In 1951 he oversaw construction of a chapel in Tok, and in 1952 a chapel was built at Delta Junction. (The Delta Junction chapel is shown in the drawing.) A chapel was also constructed at Northway.

Bingle continued his highway parish work until 1953, but the parish ministry continued until the 1960s when the Episcopal Church, with a church and priest at Tanacross, assumed responsibility for the chapels at Tok and Northway.

The old chapel at Delta Junction is now all that is left of the highway parish. No longer in use, it is located just to the north of the modern Presbyterian church, which is now operated as a joint Presbyterian/Lutheran Church.

The old chapel, constructed of spruce logs milled flat on three sides, has two rooms and is about 15' wide by 30' long. It has a low-angled gable roof with a small belfry above the front entry. The roof of the sanctuary sags a little, but the building is still in good condition and the congregation would like to preserve the building.

According to the church's current minister, Dr. Carin Björn von Letzendorf (Pastor Bear), the church had hoped to donate the old chapel to the city of Delta Junction and move it to land adjacent to Sullivan's Roadhouse. Unfortunately, those plans never came to fruition, so the congregation is studying other plans to preserve the building.

Sources:

- *Alaskan Missions, My 28 years in the Yukon Presbytery*. Rev. Bert Bingle. Self-published, no date (c 1955)
- Bert Bingle interview by Jim Cassady. 1965. Oral History Collection at the University of Alaska Fairbanks Archives
- Conversation with Rev. Dr. Carin Björn von Letzendorf, current pastor of the Delta Junction Presbyterian Faith Lutheran Church
- "The Alaska Highway Ministry." On Presbytery of the Yukon website. 1965

Richardson Highway - Big Delta

The Alaska Road Commission garage at Big Delta State Historical Park is seen as it looked in fall 2013

Big Delta ARC garage saw use until World War II

The building shown in the drawing, located at Big Delta State Historical Park to the southeast of Rika's Roadhouse, is a reconstruction of an Alaska Road Commission (ARC) garage. Of simple utilitarian design, the garage is 35' wide x 65' long. It is sheathed with rough-cut boards and has a gable roof covered in corrugated metal. The north side of the building (to the left in the drawing) has five sets of 8'-high by 10'-wide double doors, with a small 4'-high man door cut into the second set of doors. It was utilized for equipment storage in winter, and maintenance work during the summer.

I have no date for the garage's construction, but the ARC began operating a ferry across the Tanana River at Big Delta in 1905. A log cabin about 100 feet from the garage, was, according to National Park Service documents, constructed by the ARC in 1914.

The ARC used the site until 1943, when the U.S. Army commandeered the facilities. With the 1943 completion of a bridge across the Tanana just south of Big Delta, the ARC ferry was no longer needed. Rika's Roadhouse was also bypassed by the new construction, and it closed in 1947.

All the buildings at Big Delta sat abandoned until the State of Alaska acquired the property in 1976. The garage was rebuilt in the 1980s while Rika's Roadhouse and other facilities were rehabilitated.

The garage's years of service coincided with the upgrading of the Valdez-Fairbanks Trail from a rough wagon road to a highway capable of supporting motor-vehicles. This was a period of great change in Eastern Interior Alaska.

During the latter 1910s and into the 1920s the Alaska Railroad from Seward to Fairbanks was completed by the Alaska Engineering Commission (AEC); the Valdez-Fairbanks trail transitioned into the Richardson Highway; and the Washington-Alaska Military Cable and Telegraph System (WAMCATS) modernized its operations.

These three coincident events led to the ARC acquiring its own communication system. When the Alaska Railroad was built, The Alaska Engineering Commission also installed telegraph lines alongside the tracks. The WAMCATS administrators reached an agreement with the AEC to use the railroad's telegraph lines. A submarine cable already linked Seward with the Valdez WAMCATS line, so the new agreement extended WAMCATS telegraph services from Nenana to the northern Kenai Peninsula and serving points in between.

The WAMCATS had been gradually replacing its landlines with wireless telegraphy (radio) and shuttering uneconomical sections of its system. According to Morgan Blanchard's doctoral dissertation, "Wires, Wireless and Wilderness," there were only about 50 year-round residents along the road between Fairbanks and Valdez, so that segment was an obvious choice for closure.

When a new submarine cable was laid between Seward and the Lower 48 States in 1924, administrators decided to abandon the Valdez-Fairbanks line.

The ARC still needed those lines to connect its maintenance and construction camps, though. Claus-M. Naske's book, *Alaska Road Commission Historical Narrative,* states that in 1926 the 371 miles of line between Valdez and Fairbanks were transferred to the ARC. The next year the ARC extended those lines 39 miles to Chitina, and lines were extended 106 miles to Nabesna between 1930-34. It also operated a switchboard at Copper Center.

Not all segments of the line were compatible with each other, unfortunately. When telephones were first installed, it was impossible to made a direct call between Valdez and Fairbanks. The incompatible line segments met at Black Rapids Roadhouse, which had two phones--one connected to Fairbanks and one with Valdez. It was the roadhouse proprietor's job to relay messages between the two systems.

This primitive communication system lasted until World War II, when improved radio communications replaced it. Like the ARC's Big Delta garage, it had outlived its usefulness.

Sources:

- *Alaska Road Commission Historical Narrative: Final Report.* Claus-M. Naske. State of Alaska Department of Transportation. 1983
- "Big Delta Historic District nomination form – National Register of Historic Places." Janet Clemens. National Park Service. 1990
- "Wires, Wireless and Wilderness: a Sociotechnical Interpretation of Three Military Communication Stations on the Washington-Alaska Military Cable and Telegraph System (WAMCATS)." Morgan R. Blanchard. University of Nevada, Reno. Doctoral dissertation. 2010

The Timber pumping station just north of Delta Junction in 2014

Haines Pipeline supplied military fuel needs in Eastern Interior Alaska

The Haines Pipeline (also called the Haines-Fairbanks Pipeline) was a 624-mile long eight-inch-diameter line that carried fuel from Haines in Southeast Alaska to Eastern Interior Alaska military installations. It operated from 1956 to 1973.

The pipeline was successor to the World War II-era CANOL (Canadian Oil) Pipeline. The CANOL line east of Whitehorse shut down after the war. However, a four-inch Skagway-Whitehorse line and a 3-inch Whitehorse-Fairbanks line were kept in use transporting fuel brought up the Inside Passage on tankers.

Post-war military activities in Alaska outpaced the capacity of the CANOL Line, which could pump about 3,000 barrels per day (BPD). Discussions on replacing it were held as early as 1945, but planning didn't actually start until 1950.

A new pipeline was designed with a normal throughput of 9,600 BPD. It would run from the ice-free port at Haines, along the Haines Highway to Haines Junction in Canada, and then along the Alaska and Richardson Highways to Fairbanks.

This route shaved 240 miles off the Skagway-Whitehorse-Fairbanks route, and its proximity to already-developed roads allowed the use of existing bridges for pipeline crossings of rivers and streams.

The U.S. Army Corps of Engineers was responsible for construction, but private contractors performed the work. Contracts were let in October 1953 and right-of-way clearing began immediately. Bulldozers accomplished much of the work, but in some areas a seven-foot-diameter hollow steel ball filled with water was strung between tractors and dragged along the right-of-way. The filled balls weighed between 10 and 12 tons and according to reports cleared brush and trees at a rapid rate.

Once clearing was completed most of the line's pipe was laid directly on the ground. Two major sections were buried: a 40-mile section north of Haines for protection from avalanches, and a 100-mile section south of Fairbanks that crossed military maneuver areas.

The system included the pipeline itself, five pumping stations (Haines, Border, Haines Junction, Donjek, and Tok), tank farms at Haines and Tok, and a terminal facility at Haines. Normally, only the pumps at Haines, Border and Tok were used, but output could be increased to 16,500 BPD if Donjek and Haines Junction also went on-line. The line was completed in 1955 but didn't begin pumping until 1956.

Alaska's military fuel needs increased dramatically after the pipeline was completed. Fortunately, pipeline designers anticipated changes and allowed for easy modifications. In 1961, six booster stations were added to the line increasing its maximum capacity to 27,500 BPD. The new stations were constructed at Blanchard River, Destruction Bay, and Beaver in Canada; and Lakeview, Sears Creek, and Timber in the U.S.. (The drawing is of the Timber pumping station 12 miles north of Delta Junction.)

The pumping stations, isolated as they were, were self-contained communities. Living quarters were on-site, and each station had its own heating, electrical, water and sewage system. According to the U.S. Army report, "The Haines-Fairbanks Pipeline," maintaining the pipeline was considered one of the loneliest jobs someone could be assigned to.

In 1970 significant corrosion was detected along the pipeline, especially the southern half between Tok and Haines. Repair costs were prohibitive, and a study concluded that with additional fuel storage tanks at Eielson AFB and improved railroad and tanker-truck facilities, the pipeline was no longer needed.

The line's southern half was mothballed in 1971 and closed permanently in 1972. The section from Tok to Eielson was deactivated the next year. The Fairbanks-Eielson segment was used in reverse until 1992.

Most of the above-ground pipe is gone, as are the tank farms and the Haines terminal. However a few of the pumping stations (some re-purposed) can still be seen along the Richardson and Alaska Highways.

Sources:

- "Alaska's Other Pipelines." Betzi Woodman. In *Alaska Report*, Vol. 12, No. 3 (March 1971)
- "Haines-Fairbanks Pipeline: Design, Construction and Operation." D.E. Garfield, et al. U.S. Army Cold Regions Research and Engineering Laboratory. 1977
- "The Haines-Fairbanks Pipeline." Christy Hollinger. Center for Environmental Management of Military Lands. 2003

Richardson Roadhouse in the 1960s

The changing roadhouses of Richardson, Alaska

Opening and operating a roadhouse in Interior Alaska was always a gamble. A poorly chosen location could hobble a roadhouse's ability to attract travelers, or new routes might put a roadhouse miles off the main trail. Traffic along a trail could also die out completely if a gold strike faded, or a new strike lured miners elsewhere. Also, there was almost constant danger from floods, fires and other natural disasters.

Even building a roadhouse in an established community was no guarantee for success. The small community of Richardson, about 70 miles southeast of Fairbanks, is an example. The town, established in 1905 along the Valdez-Fairbanks Trail (later the Richardson Highway) on the northeast bank of the Tanana River, had three roadhouses, all apparently called the Richardson Roadhouse at one time or another.

According to Kenneth Marsh's book, *The Trail: The Story of the Historic Valdez-Fairbanks Trail that Opened Alaska's Vast Interior*, Jacob Samuelson, who operated a grocery store in early Richardson, also built the first roadhouse. Old photos show a structure built of squared logs, but little else is in known about it.

The section of the Tanana River between Big Delta and Fairbanks has one of the steepest gradients along the entire river, and the river there is turbulent, often changing course. It moved against Richardson aggressively in 1915, eating away much of the town. What was left of Richardson was forced to move, and Samuelson never rebuilt.

J. W. McClusky ran a trading post and also sold gasoline at the new townsite a mile inland along the re-aligned Richardson Highway, near Banner Creek. In 1916 he and his wife built a two-story log roadhouse just west of the creek, appropriately called McClusky's Roadhouse. In 1922, they replaced that structure with a larger flat-roofed two-story log building that could accommodate 30 guests. Their operation was renamed the Richardson Roadhouse.

With increasing traffic along the highway, McClusky expanded the business again. He added a two-story section to the end of the roadhouse, doubling its size. Unfortunately, he evidently overbuilt, and the anticipated tourists never materialized.

McClusky eventually closed the roadhouse and his name disappeared from the history books. The building sat vacant for several years and was eventually disassembled, moved to Fairbanks, and re-assembled as a warehouse. The roadhouse's disappearance may have coincided with the town's second relocation away from the turbulent river during the 1920s.

Fred Wilkins, who was a homesteader in the area, built the third roadhouse at Richardson's second location in about 1915. When the town moved a third time, he relocated his roadhouse to the north side of the highway. After McClusky closed his operation, Wilkins renamed his business the Richardson Roadhouse.

The drawing shows this third roadhouse as it looked in about 1960. The log structure, with false front, was divided into two sections — a café on one side, and liquor store/convenience store on the other. Behind and to the sides of the roadhouse were several out buildings including barn and storage sheds. To the right of the roadhouse were small guest cabins (later replaced by a small motel unit). On the left were gas pumps, several small frame buildings used for automotive service, and a log garage.

The roadhouse was located approximately halfway between Fort Wainwright in Fairbanks, and Fort Greely just south of Delta Junction. It was a convenient rest stop for Army buses shuttling soldiers between the two posts, and old photos show the buses parked in front of the roadhouse.

The structure containing the café and store burned down in 1982. The convenience store moved into one of the tiny frame buildings next to the garage and gas pumps, and, along with the motel unit, the roadhouse struggled on for a few more years before closing permanently. Now the only building remaining is the weathered log garage.

Sources:

- Fairbanks North Star Borough Property Records
- *Historic Resources in the Fairbanks North Star Borough*. Janet Matheson & F. Bruce Haldeman. Fairbanks North Star Borough, 1981
- *Roadhouses of the Richardson Highway*. Walter T. Phillips. Alaska History Commission, 1985
- *The Trail: The Story of the Historic Valdez-Fairbanks Trail that Opened Alaska's Vast Interior*. Kenneth Marsh. Trapper Creek Museum, 2008

Denali National Park and Preserve - Muldrow Glacier

Stearman C3B, registration number NC5415, on Muldrow Glacier in 1932

1928 Stearman biplane made Alaska aviation history

The plane in the drawing is a 1928 Stearman C3B, registration number NC5415. It is, along with planes such as Ben Eielson's World War I-era Curtis Wright JN-4 (on display at Fairbanks International Airport), and the 1931 Fairchild Pilgrim 100 at the Alaska Aviation Heritage Museum in Anchorage, a rare and iconic piece of Alaska aviation history.

In the ten years that this plane flew in Alaska, NC5415 was piloted by several famous pioneer Alaskan aviators, including Noel Wien, Ben Eielson, Harold Gillam, Joe Crosson and Merle Smith.

Manufactured by the Stearman Aircraft Corporation of Wichita, Kansas, it actually began life in 1928 as a C2B, the second model manufactured by the company.

It originally had a Wright J4 nine-cylinder radial engine. However, by 1932 the plane had been upgraded to Stearman's C3B model. The upgrade included replacing the engine with the more powerful Wright J5 nine-cylinder radial engine.

The J5, after it was developed, quickly earned a reputation as an extremely reliable engine. Charles Lindbergh's plane, the "Spirit of St. Louis," had a J5 engine when he made his solo non-stop flight across the Atlantic Ocean in 1927.

According to a 1980 article by Les Kares, who restored the plane, it was shipped to Alaska in 1928. During its first few years in Alaska, it was flown by Harold Gillam in the 1929 search for aviator Ben Eielson, who had crashed off the coast of Siberia. It was also flown by Joe Crosson in January 1931, when he flew the NC5415 from Fairbanks to Barrow over the uncharted Brooks Range to deliver diphtheria antitoxin.

In 1932, it was used in a series of firsts for both aviation and Denali National Park and Preserve. Planes had been used to supply the mining camp of Kantishna, on the far side of Denali, since the mid 1920s, and sightseeing flights around the mountain became increasingly popular about 1930.

However, as explained by Dirk Tordoff in his 1994 article, "Airplanes on Denali," no plane had landed on the mountain before 1932, although by that time, mountaineers had become interested in using planes to photograph and map potential climbing routes.

That year, an expedition climbed the lower portions of the mountain to conduct cosmic ray experiments, and Alaskan Airways, the Stearman's owners, delivered the expedition's personnel and scientific equipment to the 5,600-foot level of Muldrow Glacier, near the mountain's base.

Alaskan Airways made several trips to the glacier for the Cosmic Ray Expedition. Pilot Joe Crosson landed the first plane on Denali, a Fairchild 71, on April 25th. The Stearman, piloted by Jerry Jones, was the second plane to land on May 3rd.

On May 16th, Jones returned to the glacier in NC5415 to rescue an expedition member who was seriously ill with high-altitude pulmonary edema.

The earlier flights to Denali, with ski-equipped planes, had taken off and landed on still-frozen Birch Lake. That was impossible by mid-May, so, Weeks Field's dirt runway was deliberately flooded so Jones could take off and land on its muddy surface. The flight was successful – the first air rescue from Denali.

Later in 1932, Alaskan Airways was acquired by Pacific Alaska Airways (a subsidiary of Pan American Airways). Pacific Alaska eventually sold NC5415, and it ended up in the fleet of Cordova Air Service, where Merle Smith worked as a pilot. Smith was piloting this plane when he earned his "Mudhole Smith" nickname.

NC5415 crashed in a remote section of the Wrangell Mountains in 1939. Due to the crash site's inaccessibility, the wreck sat in the mountains for almost 30 years until being air-lifted by helicopter to Gulkana.

It was acquired in 1968 by Seattle aviation buff, Les Kares, who, over the next ten years, restored the plane to flying condition.

It is now owned by Alaska Aviation Heritage Museum in Anchorage, and is on display at its Lake Hood location.

Sources:

- "Adventures of an Alaskan biplane." Les and Janet Kares. In *Alaska Magazine*. December 1980
- "Airplanes on Denali." Dirk Tordoff. In *Alaska History*. Vol. 9, No. 2, Fall, 1994
- Alaska Aviation Museum website, alaskaairmuseum.org
- Photographs from the Crosson Family Papers. In the University of Alaska, Fairbanks Archives

1924 Fageol Safety Bus at Mt. McKinley National Park in the 1930s, from historical photo

The Fageol Safety Bus and the Denali Park Road

Buses have ferried Denali National Park and Preserve (originally Mt. McKinley National Park) visitors into the park for more than 80 years. The Fageol Safety Bus shown in the drawing (the most modern bus of its time in the 1920s) was one of the first generation of buses used in the park. The drawing is based on a 1930's photograph showing the bus in service at the park.

Mt. McKinley National Park was created in 1917 but did not receive any funding from the federal government until 1921. It then took several years for park superintendent Harry Karstens to establish park headquarters at Riley Creek.

According to Jane Bryant's book, *Snapshots from the Past: A Roadside History of Denali National Park and*

Preserve, once the Alaska Railroad reached the park and the park's headquarters had been established, efforts turned to developing access for visitors.

The Alaska Road Commission (ARC), the federal agency responsible for building roads in the territory, was interested in building a road from the railroad at the park entrance, to the Kantishna mining district on the far side of the park. The Park Service wanted access into the park.

Both purposes could be served by one road, so the road commission and Park Service entered into an agreement to build a 90-mile road across the park. According to Bryant's book, the ARC constructed the road, but the Park Service provided most of the project's funding.

Reconnaissance and clearing of the road right-of-way were accomplished in 1921-22. Actual construction started in 1923 and was completed in 1938.

The miles of road built annually was small, but the ARC faced severe challenges during construction. Funding for the project came piecemeal and often constrained how much work could be done in a season. Equipment, supplies and workers had to be brought in by railroad, and once in the field, the ARC faced a short construction season; difficult terrain, including permafrost; and often inclement weather

If the ARC alone had been responsible for building the road, the route would have been based just on practicability — getting from the railroad to Kantishna in an expedient manner. The Park Service, however, was also interested in the visitor experience, and on at least on one occasion convinced the road commission to alter the road's route.

The ARC had planned to route the road east of the West Fork Toklat River over a low pass to the main Toklat River. The Park Service preferred the road take a higher pass with sweeping panoramic vistas. The new route was more difficult to build. However, without the change, park visitors would not now be able to travel over Polychrome Pass.

The Savage River was the park's primary visitor destination until McKinley Park Hotel was constructed. The park's first concessionaire, Mt. McKinley Tourist and Transportation Company (MMT&TC) constructed a camp at Savage River and ran busses into the park from the railroad. (At that time there was no road to the park. All vehicles had to be shipped in via the Alaska Railroad.)

Bobby Sheldon, the first person to drive from Fairbanks to Valdez over the Valdez-Fairbanks Trail, was the MMT&TC's general manager. As part of his manager duties he was responsible for a fleet of vehicles.

One of those vehicles was the 1924 Fageol bus. Information from the Fountainhead Antique Auto Museum, which renovated the bus in 2014, states that in 1928 the MMT&TC bought the used bus in Seattle and shipped it to Alaska. It ran the park road until the mid-1930s, when the bus was retired and put into storage.

The MMT&TC lost its concession in 1941, and the Alaska Railroad bought MMT&TC's equipment. The bus was then brought to Fairbanks and sat neglected for more than 70 years. That is when owner Diane Dawson donated it to the auto museum. The museum renovated the bus for display, and it can now be viewed at McKinley Chalet Resort at McKinley Village along the Parks Highway.

Sources:

- "A Fageol Safety Coach is Rescued." Nancy DeWitt. Fountainhead Antique Auto Museum blog (http://fountainheadauto.blogspot.com). 9-10-2014
- Signage at McKinley Chalet Resort
- "Historic coach goes on display in Denali area," Kris Capps. In *Fairbanks Daily News-Miner*. 6-18-2015
- Photo from Harry and Norma Hoght Papers. University of Alaska, Anchorage - Archives
- *Snapshots from the Past: A Roadside history of Denali National Park and Preserve*. Jane Bryant. National Park Service. 2011

Denali National Park and Preserve - Headquarters Site

Built in 1926, the superintendent's cabin at Denali National Park and Preserve is the oldest Park Service-built cabin in the park

Superintendent's office is one of oldest buildings at Denali National Park

According to Jane Bryant's book, *Snapshots from the Past, a Roadside History of Denali National Park and Preserve*, in 1914 a frontier settlement coalesced near the present-day visitor center (at that time outside the park) at Denali National Park and Preserve.

The community, eventually called McKinley Park Station, initially served prospectors, hunters and trappers. After the Alaska Engineering Commission erected a small depot and built a camp to support construction of the Riley Creek railroad bridge (completed in 1922), the community boomed.

Enterprising individuals, eager to capitalize on the railroad's presence and the newly-created park, established businesses on benches above Riley and Hines Creeks near the depot. Several roadhouses, restaurants and trading posts operated there.

The land around the depot, except for the railroad right-of-way, was eventually absorbed into the park, but when Harry Karstens, the park's first superintendent, arrived in 1921, the best land was already claimed. Karstens had to build park headquarters near the confluence of Riley and Hines Creeks, where it was damp, prone to flooding, and extremely cold during winter.

Karstens, dissatisfied with the site, tried fruitlessly to move headquarters closer to the depot. In 1924 he opted to move away from the railroad entirely.

Construction on the park road had begun in 1923, and Karstens decided park headquarters should be along that road. In a 1924 letter to the Park Service director he described a site just west of Rock Creek that he hoped to move to. "There is a beautiful spot, with ample room for expansion, one and two-thirds miles from the railroad... Building headquarters at this point will simplify the work of checking persons entering the park or leaving it."

Approval came in February 1925, and Karstens and his rangers began moving that summer. With no relocation funds available, their early efforts centered on erecting buildings at the new site using salvaged materials from the Riley Creek site and the abandoned railroad construction camp. None of those buildings survive.

The superintendent's office (shown in the drawing) was built in 1926 adjacent to the park road. The one-room, 20'6" by 19'6" single-story cabin is built of locally-cut, peeled spruce logs. It has a low-gabled roof covered with metal roofing, with the gable extending over an 8'-deep front porch. The cabin's double six-lite windows are similar to those in other cabins constructed during that period.

The cabin served as the superintendent's office until 1941, when it was converted into the first park museum. The building was moved a short distance south to the headquarters utility area in 1950, and in 1952 it was moved to the north side of the park road. It was converted to employee housing in 1960.

At some point the gable extension over the front porch was cut back and replaced with a shed roof. After the cabin became a residence, a room was added at the rear.

During renovations of the cabin between 2013 and 2016, the addition was removed, and the drywall and studs were pulled from the cabin's interior walls. The revealed logs had been hand-hewn flat on their interior side and were still in good condition Also discovered were items like old uniform scraps used as chinking.

Unwilling to re-cover the interior log work, and because of the cabin's association with Karstens and its significance as the oldest surviving headquarters building, the Park Service changed plans and restored the cabin to its original appearance. This included rebuilding the gable extension over the front porch. The Park Service also moved the cabin to a site more accessible to visitors, next to the park's administrative offices south of the park road, all in time for Denali National Park and Preserve's 2017 centennial.

Sources:

- *A History of Mount McKinley National Park Alaska*. Grant H. Pearson. National Park Service. 1953
- Correspondence with Erik Johnson, historian at Denali National Park and Preserve
- *Crown Jewel of the North: An Administrative History of Denali National Park and Preserve, Volume I*. Frank Norris. National Park Service. 2006
- "Mount McKinley National Park Headquarters District, National Register of Historic Places Nomination Form." Gail Evans. National Park Service. 1987
- "Park staff fight to preserve cabin hand built by Denali's first superintendent 90 years ago." Erin Kirkland. In *Anchorage Daily News*. 6-19-2016
- *Snapshots from the Past, A Roadside History of Denali National Park and Preserve*. Jane Bryant. National Park Service. 2011

The old warehouse (now offices) at Denali National Park and Preserve headquarters as it looks today

Denali National Park warehouse changes function but still serves

The first headquarters site for Mount McKinley National Park (now Denali National Park and Preserve) was on low-lying ground near the confluence of Riley and Hines creeks. This site was subject to flooding and very cold during winter. In 1924 Harry Karstens, the park's first superintendent, decided to move his headquarters to a better location.

National Park Service documents describe Karstens' proposed headquarters site as a "gently sloping forested terrace just north of Hines Creek." (Hines Creek is a tributary of Riley Creek, which in turn flows into the Nenana River.)

In a letter to the NPS director, Karstens stated that the site had "ample room for expansion," and, being situated next to the road into the park, would "simplify the work of checking persons entering the park or leaving it."

Karstens and his rangers wasted no time dismantling several structures at the first headquarters and reusing the materials to build anew at the Hines Creek site. Between 1925 and 1927 nine structures were built there. Designed and built by rangers, the structures were constructed of logs and rough-sawn lumber. Only one structure, the old superintendent's office, survives from this period.

Beginning in 1928, new park buildings were designed by NPS landscape architects. These architects designed in a "rustic" style, using local building materials and construction methods to harmonize the buildings with the Interior Alaska landscape. By 1935, 18 structures had been constructed at the new headquarters site.

The building shown in the drawing, located adjacent to the current Denali National Park and Preserve administration building at headquarters, is the first architect-designed structure built at Mount McKinley National Park. When constructed in 1928 it was an unheated warehouse.

The 32' by 32', 1 1/2-story structure is built of peeled spruce logs, saddle-notched at the corners. It has a gabled roof.

Jane Bryant's book, *Snapshots from the Past, A Roadside History of Denali National Park and Preserve*, relates that the NPS procured the logs itself, floating them three miles down a "nearby" creek to the park road. From there an old Alaska Road Commission tractor was used to skid most of the logs to the construction site. The tractor gave up the ghost before the final logs were transported.

Construction on the warehouse proceeded during the summer of 1928, and most work was completed by winter. Finish work such as installing doors and windows was accomplished that winter.

The warehouse had a loading dock and double freight doors on the southern side of the building, 16-lite casement window units centered in the east, north and west walls, and a pedestrian door at the northwest corner of the west wall. The building originally had a wood foundation and rolled roofing.

It served as a warehouse for over 50 years. In 1982 a concrete foundation was installed, the then metal roofing was replaced with wood shakes, and the building converted to office space. The loading dock was removed and the freight doors replaced with a wood-frame wall-insert with a two-lite casement window. The east- and north-side multi-lite windows were replaced with modern windows, and the west-side window was replaced by another pedestrian door plus a small window.

When I visited in 2011, the facade had been returned to its original configuration: windows replaced with multi-lite ones similar to the originals, the west-side central door removed, the loading dock rebuilt (but reduced in width), and the south-side wall insert replaced with a wall replicating the appearance of the original freight doors (with the addition of large windows).

The building is part of the Mount McKinley National Park Headquarters District, which was added to the National Register of Historic Places in 1987.

Sources:

- "Mount McKinley National Park Headquarters District, National Register of Historic Places Nomination Form." Gail Evans. National Park Service. 1987
- *Snapshots from the Past, A Roadside History of Denali National Park and Preserve.* Jane Bryant. National Park Service. 2011
- "Warehouse, Mt. McKinley Park Headquarters Historic District," photos, plans and drawings. Historic American Building Survey, National Park Service. 1986

Ebb and flow of mining at Kantishna reflected in Eldorado Creek history

The Comstock Cabin on Eldorado Creek in 1994. This cabin was built in the 1950s.

Kantishna's Eldorado Creek, as opposed to the 26 other Eldorado Creeks listed in the *Dictionary of Alaska Place Names*, is a 5.5-mile-long tributary of Moose Creek, located just downstream from the confluence of Moose and Eureka creeks. Mined since the short-lived 1905-06 Kantishna gold rush, Eldorado Creek's mining history is a microcosm of the ebb and flow of mineral development in the Kantishna area.

During the brief six months the Kantishna gold rush lasted, lode deposits of silver were discovered along Eldorado Creek, as well as a stibnite deposit (an ore of antimony) on Slate Creek, an Eldorado Creek tributary near its headwaters.

Mining picked up again during World War I. Slate Creek's stibnite deposit was worked between 1915 and 1918, the Kantishna Hydraulic Mining Company mined along Moose Creek as far south as the mouth of Eldorado Creek until about 1922, and a silver deposit at the head of Eldorado Creek produced ore through 1923.

Along with other Kantishna mines, those along Eldorado Creek were hampered by high transportation costs, as a road from the Alaska Railroad to Kantishna was not completed until

1939. Most mines, even those with rich deposits, were simply uneconomical to operate.

World War II brought gold and silver mining at Kantishna to a standstill, as it did elsewhere in Alaska, since the two metals were not vital for the war effort. However, stibnite was considered strategic (since antimony was used in munitions) and from 1942 to 1944 it was mined at Slate Creek. During the war, a tractor road was pushed up Eldorado to Slate Creek.

Gold and silver mining resumed after World War II. Johnny Busia, who lived at Kantishna since 1918, opened the Comstock claims along the middle section of Eldorado Creek. At his claim he built the 12' by 16' wood-frame cabin shown in the drawing, now known as the Comstock cabin. Busia drove at least one adit (a horizontal entrance into a mine) into the hillside behind the cabin searching for silver. He later sold the claims to Frank Bonnell (relationship to me unknown) who excavated several more adits before abandoning the mine.

In 1959, Dan Ashbrook moved into the Kantishna area. He settled in to the Eldorado Creek area, acquiring 180 acres of patented claims. During a visit with him in 1994, he told me that he mined the lower portions of Eldorado Creek with a "dry-land dredge." Although I did not ask him specifics, dry-land dredges usually consist of a tracked excavator trailed by a mobile washing plant. Kantishna's remoteness and shallow gravels played to these dredges' strengths — small size, portability and economical operation, without being hampered by their limited excavating depths.

Dan also related that when antimony was mined at Slate Creek in the early 1970s and again in the early 1980s (dependent on fluctuating metal prices) the road up Eldorado Creek was so smooth that he could drive his Cadillac all the way to the top. Mining at Slate Creek stopped in 1983, and in the following decade the mining road rapidly deteriorated. By the time I hiked it in 1994, much of it was just a rough trail along the creek bottom.

Recently, gold mining resumed along Eldorado Creek. After the 1980 expansion of Denali National Park to include the Kantishna Hills, and a subsequent 1985 lawsuit, mining ceased. Valid mining claims were not extinguished, though. The Park Service bought most of these claims, but in 2016, a plan of operation was approved for a suction-dredge operation on the last remaining unpatented mining claims within the park, along the middle section of Eldorado Creek near the Comstock cabin.

Sources:

- Conversations with Dan Ashbrook, Kantishna resident. 1994
- Conversation with Dave Shirokauer, Lead Science and Resource Team Leader, Denali National Park and Preserve. 2018
- *Crown Jewel of the North, an Administrative History of Denali National Park and Preserve, Volume 2, Chapter 14: Mining and Kantishna Area Management.* Frank Norris. National Park Service. 2006
- *Dictionary of Alaska Place Names.* Donald Orth. U.S.G.S. 1967
- "Eldorado Creek Mining Plan of Operations Environmental Assessment," Steve Carwile, Britta Schroeder, & Linda Stromquist. National Park Service. May 2016
- Mindat.org mineralogical database — entries for Alpha and Comstock silver mines on Eldorado Creek, and Slate Creek stibnite mine

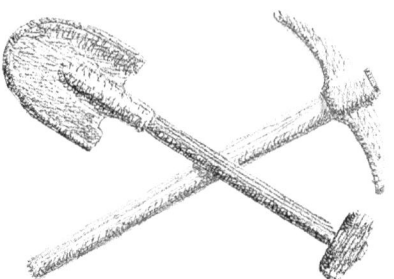

The tipple at Suntrana is seen here how it looked in about 2005. Healy Creek is to the right of the tipple. The entrance to Suntrana Coal Mine, now sealed, was to the left, just outside the picture. The winding road in the background is Healy Spur Road.

Suntrana Coal Mine, near Healy, is just a memory

Suntrana, near Healy, takes its name from an Athabascan word meaning "burning hills," denoting the smoke rising from smoldering coal seams nearby.

Besides Usibelli Coal Mine, the area is best-known for the old Suntrana townsite and underground coal mine in the narrow Healy Creek valley, just upstream from Suntrana Creek and 2.5 miles east of Healy. The Healy River Coal Corporation opened its mine there in 1921.

In the mine's first year of operation, coal was hauled by tractor-drawn wagons to the Nenana River and by tram across the river to the Alaska Railroad (ARR). In 1922, the ARR built a bridge over the river and a spur line to the mine. In addition to coal trains, the mine ran a "doodlebug" (an automobile equipped to run on rails) to ferry people between Suntrana and Healy.

In 1922, Austin "Cap" Lathrop began investing in the mine, and by 1924 he was its principal stockholder and president. Under his management, the mine grew into the largest coal producer in Interior Alaska.

The mine's portal was at the base of the hills just north of Healy Creek. All mining activities were restricted to that side of the creek.

Initially, most workers lived in bunkhouses at the mine. Later, log cabins were built on company-controlled land south of the creek to house families of married workers. From those log cabins sprang the company town of Suntrana. Over time, Suntrana expanded to include numerous wood-frame residences, a few mobile homes, a one-room school, company store, recreation hall and commissary, and two churches.

According to the *Dictionary of Alaska Place Names*, in 1930 Suntrana had a population of 69, and by 1950 had expanded to 150 residents. A 1950s map shows about two-dozen structures in the town and about a dozen across the creek at the mine.

Cap Lathrop died in an accident at the mine in 1950, and a group of Anchorage investors bought the Suntrana mine in 1953. Usibelli Coal Company, interested in Suntrana's coal loading facility, bought the operation in 1961. A year later, they closed the underground mine.

In 1967 Usibelli constructed a new tipple (shown in the drawing) at Suntrana to load coal into railroad cars. That same year, the railroad bridge over the Nenana River was planked, finally allowing workers and their families to drive themselves across the river.

Mine workers continued living at Suntrana, but Usibelli's expanding operations soon forced it to find alternative employee housing. Workers began migrating toward the Parks highway after is was completed in 1972. Usibelli leased state land near the highway and subleased lots to its workers. The Suntrana townsite was shuttered, and many of its buildings were moved to Healy.

Rolfe Buzzell's report, *Mining the Burning Hills*, states that Usibelli relocated all its Suntrana operations to the Poker Flats area, near the Nenana River northwest of Suntrana, in 1983, and the old Suntrana coal lease was transferred to the State of Alaska. In 1986 the surviving structures at the Suntrana townsite were removed as part of a mine reclamation project. A year later, in the manner of the proverbial farmer closing the barn door after the horse had escaped, the state legislature declared the area a State Historic Site.

The tipple and a few associated buildings were all that remained. In 2000, the Alaska Office of History and Archeology determined that the tipple was not eligible for inclusion on the National Register of Historic Places. Coupled with the tipple's deteriorating condition and site contamination from industrial pollutants, the state removed the remaining buildings in 2008.

Now, where once a vibrant little community stood, nothing is left but dusty, overgrown roads.

Sources:

- *Alaska's first Homegrown Millionaire, Life and Times of Cap Lathrop*. Elizabeth Tower. Publication Consultants. 2006
- Conversations with McKenzie Johnson, archeologist; and Jo Antonson, State Historian, at the Alaska State Office of History and Archeology. 2018
- *Mining the Burning Hills: a History of Alaska's Suntrana Coal Mine and Townsite*. Rolfe Buzzell. Office of History and Archeology, Alaska Division of Parks and Outdoor Recreation. 1994.
- "Site Report: ADNR Suntrana Mine Site." Alaska Department of Environmental Conservation. 2017
- "Usibelli Coal Mine History." Usibelli Coal Mine website, http://www.usibelli.com. 2015

The Mears Memorial Bridge in Nenana is seen here as it looked in late winter 1923 when the temporary piling beneath the bridge was still in place. The drawing is based on a photograph in the archives at the Anchorage Museum.

Mears Memorial Bridge the final link in the Alaska Railroad

By 1921 the Alaska Railroad was tantalizingly close to completion. The 470 miles of track that would carry trains between Seward on the Kenai Peninsula and Fairbanks in Interior Alaska was essentially complete. The only hindrance was a 700-foot gap across the Tanana River that took an additional two years to bridge.

For seven years the Alaska Engineering Commission (AEC), the federal agency responsible for constructing the railway, had been rebuilding the dilapidated Alaska Northern Railroad line from Seward to the head of Turnagain Arm, extending tracks northward to the Susitna Valley and on through Broad Pass to Nenana, and building depots and other support facilities. By 1921 the line between Seward and Nenana was complete.

As part of its construction efforts, the AEC had purchased the bankrupt Tanana Valley Railroad (TVRR) in 1917. After acquiring the line, the AEC ran tracks southward from Fairbanks to the north bank of the Tanana River, across from Nenana.

When the Tanana was ice-free the AEC provided ferry service across the river. It operated numerous boats during construction to transport passengers, freight and building materials across the river. After freeze-up, when winter ice was thick enough, the AEC laid railroad tracks over the river ice to the south shore.

Before a bridge at Nenana could be built, a lengthy inclined wooden trestle (later replaced by earthwork) was constructed up to bridge height, and a 420' steel-truss viaduct was erected from the trestle to the south pier of the bridge. (The trestle separated Nenana's Native village from the white man's town, and the viaduct allowed passage beneath it between the two communities.) Both the approach trestle and viaduct were completed by August of 1922.

The bridge across the river was constructed in 1922-23. It was designed by Ralph Modjeski, a Polish-born American civil engineer who was one of the pre-eminent bridge designers of that era. Modjeski was directly or indirectly involved with the design and construction of almost 40 bridges scattered across the United States, including the Mid-Hudson Bridge in Pougkeepsie, NY, and the San Francisco-Oakland Bay Bridge.

The Tanana River bridge was fabricated and assembled by the American Bridge Company. When built, the 700'-long single-truss steel bridge was the longest truss span in the United States. Matthew Reckard's 1999 article about the bridge in the *Ester Republic* states that it is still the third-longest simple truss in the nation and the longest span of any kind in Alaska.

Modjeski was a pioneer in using reinforced concrete for bridgework. Numerous small piers to support the viaduct and two massive piers to support the bridge were formed of poured concrete, five years before Cap Lathrop built the first poured concrete building in Fairbanks.

With the bridge piers completed by October of 1922, workers sank pilings into the river bottom to support a wooden falsework trestle across the river. The falsework, brought up to bridge height, is what supported the steel railbed as it was constructed and as the truss-work above was added.

By January of 1923 the new bridge was essentially completed, including wooden decking and rails. The first train rolled across the bridge on February 9th, 1923.

With completion of the bridge, President Warren G. Harding traveled to Alaska to drive in the ceremonial golden spike at mile 413.7 of the Alaska Railroad, at the north end of the bridge.

According to an article on the AlaskaRails.Org website, on July 15th of 1923 Territorial Governor Scott Bone inserted the 14-carat spike into a pre-drilled hole and President Harding tapped it home. The spike was then replaced with a regular iron spike. The golden spike was presented to Colonel Frederick Mears, chairman and chief engineer of the AEC (and the bridge's namesake).

Sources:

- Alaska Engineering Commission photographs of Tanana River bridge construction. Anchorage Museum of History & Art. Library & Archives
- "Golden Spike." John Combs. On AlaskaRails.Org website. 1997
- *Railroad in the Clouds: The Alaska Railroad in the Age of Steam, 1914-1945*. William H. Wilson. Pruett Publishing. 1977
- *Tanana Valley Railroad, the Gold Dust Line*. Nicholas Deely. Denali Designs. 1996
- "The Mears Memorial Bridge." Matthew Reckard. in the *Ester Republic*. 1999

Rusty Heurlin's studio in Ester in the early winter of 2017

Ester studio evokes memory of painter, Rusty Heurlin

The cabin in the drawing was the studio for Alaska painter, Magnus Colcord "Rusty" Heurlin. Matthew Reckard, the artist's neighbor, recently showed me Rusty's studio.

Located on Main Street in Ester, the simple, gable-roofed log-cabin studio was built in 1965, replacing a studio Rusty constructed when he moved to Ester. (Judy Gumm, long-time Ester resident, told me that another well-known Alaskan painter, Ted Lambert, lived in Rusty's old studio for a while.)

Rusty was born to Swedish-American parents at Christianstad, Sweden in 1895, and was raised in Wakefield, Massachusetts. He attended Fenway School of Illustration in Boston for a year after high school.

Then, craving adventure, he worked his way west, eventually sailing to Alaska in 1916. Landing at Valdez, he spent a winter living in Sydney Laurence's old studio. (Laurence moved to Anchorage in 1915.)

The United States entered World War I in April 1917, and Rusty left Alaska to enlist in the U.S. Navy. After he demobilized in 1919, Rusty enrolled at New York City's Grand Central School of Art.

In 1921 he began illustrating stories for pulp magazines such as *Adventure, Sky Birds,* and *Top-Notch*. According to the website, Field Guide to Wild American Pulp Artists, Rusty took a hiatus from illustrating in 1922, returning to Alaska to study Inupiat culture in the Point Barrow area.

He returned to the East Coast in 1923 and resumed illustrating magazines. The influence of his Alaskan studies can be seen in many of his illustrations. It was as a story illustrator that he honed his skills for story-telling through his paintings.

During the 1930s, the Great Depression, coupled with advances in photographic reproduction and the advent of color photography, ended many illustrators' careers. Rusty was no exception. By 1933 magazine commissions had dried up, and Rusty sought refuge with the Work's Progress Administration's Federal Arts Project.

Deciding that he could starve in Alaska just as well as he could on the East Coast, Rusty moved back to Alaska in 1935. Once here, he worked any honest job he could find—as miner, fisherman, and laborer on the Alaska Railroad. He also spent four seasons on Inupiat whaling crews along the Arctic coast. And all the while he snuck in his art studies.

When the U.S. declared war on Japan in 1942, Rusty volunteered for the Alaska Territorial Guard. According to a 1945 issue of the magazine, *Alaska Life*, Captain Heurlin was in Barrow during an influenza outbreak and helped distribute sulfa tablets to villagers, handing out so many pills that the Inupiat called them "Rusty's pills."

Rusty settled in Ester, just outside Fairbanks, after the war, got married, continued to paint, and began teaching art classes at the University of Alaska (the first art classes offered at the U). He eventually left the university to devote more time to painting, but continued to teach privately. One of his students was Fairbanks artist, Ray Sandberg.

Much of his effort after leaving the university was focused on producing several series of "story-telling" murals. One of those was "The Big Stampede"—15 murals depicting the gold rush history of the Yukon and Alaska. Those murals are on display at the Pioneer Museum in Pioneer Park in Fairbanks.

He completed two other series: "Our Heritage," reflecting the development of Inupiat culture; and "The Great Land," showing Alaska's history from Russian America to statehood.

Murals from "Our Heritage" used to greet visitors at the Fairbanks airport passenger terminal. Unfortunately, most of his murals except the "Big Stampede" series are now in storage at the University of Alaska.

Rusty died in 1986 but his legacy lives on through his art. If you do go searching for his studio, remember that it is on private property

Sources:

- "Colcord Heurlin." David Saunders. From *Field Guide to Wild American Pulp Artists* website, www.pulpartists.com. 2015
- Conversation with Judy Gum and Matthew Reckard, both long-time Ester residents and Rusty Heurlin's neighbors. 2017
- Fairbanks North Star Borough property records
- "Heurlin Paints History." Jimmy Bedford. In *Alaska Today* magazine. 1984, V. 12
- "Northern Lights." No author. In *Alaska Life: The Territorial Magazine*. April 1945
- "Teacher and Student reunite through Art." Donna Redhead Sandberg. In F*airbanks Daily News-Miner*. 2-11-1996

Elliot Highway - Livengood

Old Horse Barn in Livengood. Horses were a primary means of hauling freight to Livengood during the camp's early years.

The Tolovana Tram, early Livengood's jury-rigged transport system

Jay Livengood and Teddy Hudson discovered gold in the headwaters of the Tolovana River in 1914, leading to a minor gold rush in 1915. The resulting camp (eventually named Livengood) was remote, even though it was only 80 miles northeast of Fairbanks. With no established trails into the area, during the camp's early years the surest way to transport freight and passengers was by boat via the Tolovana River, a tributary of the Tanana.

The Tolovana River was not the swiftest route, though. According to a 1924 report by the federal Board of Engineers for Rivers and Harbors, as the raven flies the distance from the Tolovana's mouth to its headwaters is only 55 miles. However, the Tolovana is tortuously twisting, so by water the distance is 175 miles.

Complicating the journey was "Log Jam," a 1½-mile section of river 125 water-miles above the Tolovana's mouth. The river doubled back on its course at that point, and three distinct jams blocked transportation. Each jam consisted of interlaced logs filling the channel from the bottom of the river bed to several feet above high water. Silted in and covered with grass, the jams dammed the river, with a 5.1-foot difference in water level between the log jam's upper and lower ends.

Freight and passengers had to be portaged across the isthmus of the river bend and reloaded on to smaller boats, then transported by river another 40 to 50 miles to a point where goods could be freighted by horse to Livengood.

Cleona Erickson moved to Livengood in 1915. Audrey Parker, in her book, *Livengood, The Last Stampede*, published portions of Erickson's diary in which she records a 20-day boat trip from Fairbanks to Livengood, 18 of those days spent ascending the Tolovana.

Entrepreneurs quickly began making improvements to the Tolovana route. By the end of 1915 two short trams had been constructed across Log Jam isthmus, and work started on a 13-mile tramway from Trappers Cabin (about 40 miles above Log Jam) to Livengood.

The tramway consisted of wooden 4" by 4" "rails" placed on top of moss. On top of those rails ran a Dodge touring car riding on tireless, flanged steel wheels; pulling three trailers (also with flanged wheels), each capable of carrying 1½ tons. According to government reports, the tramway crossed one slough, three swamp lakes and a branch of the West Fork River.

Of course, the river route was only open during the summer, and overland trails were blazed to provide winter access. Those overland trails crossed marshy areas and could only be traversed during winter. Due to the time, labor and equipment required for shipping via the Tolovana River, the winter trails proved much less costly for freighting.

Finished in 1916, the Tolovana Tram was privately-operated until 1924, when the federal government assumed operation. The government operated the tram until 1930. By then most freight was shipped via winter trail, and Livengood residents, tired of the tram's high rates, petitioned the Alaska Road Commission (ARC) to build an all-season road between Fairbanks and Livengood.

The ARC agreed. It closed the tram and began work on upgrading the Olnes-to-Livengood trail to automobile standards. By 1938 the Elliott Highway had been completed between Olnes and Livengood. The tramway itself, being of wooden construction, quickly rotted away and there is no trace of it today.

The drawing depicts the old horse barn in Livengood. Although apparently not directly associated with the Tolovana Tram, the barn is a reminder of the community's earliest days, when pack horses, horse-drawn wagons, sledges and boats, and rudimentary transportation systems like the Tolovana Tram linked Livengood with the outside world.

Sources:

- "Letter from the Secretary of War, With a Letter from the Chief of Engineers, Reports on Preliminary Examination and Survey of Tolovana River, Alaska." 68th Congress. 1924
- *Livengood: The Last Stampede*. Audrey E. Parker. Hats Off Books. 2003
- "The Gold Placers of the Tolovana District." J.B. Mertie Jr.. In *The Mineral Resources of Alaska*. U.S. Government Printing Office. 1916

Warehouse at Livengood, constructed by Livengood Placer, Inc. as it looks today

Livengood Placers and its vagabond gold dredge

The building depicted in the drawing is an old warehouse near Livengood. Of heavy timber-frame construction, it has ship-lap siding (except for the gable ends which are board-and-batten), a metal roof and is painted blue. About 40-feet-wide and 80-feet-long, there are offices/workshops located on one end, a large parts room in the middle and an even larger storage area at the far end.

The warehouse is in remarkable condition considering how long it has sat vacant. It is one of the last remnants of Livengood Placer's two-decade-long struggle to develop and operate a gold-dredging operation just north of Livengood.

Clark Spence's book, *The Northern Gold Fleet*, states that in 1924, a Livengood mining engineer tried to interest the Fairbanks Exploration Company (FE Co.), which was bringing dredges to the Fairbanks area, into expanding its operations to Livengood. Those talks never came to fruition.

Not until 1934 did Outside interests pay attention to Livengood and conduct tests that showed the potential for profitable gold-dredging. In 1936, Goldfield Mines of Reno acquired an interest in Livengood claims, formed Livengood Placers, Inc., and began construction of a dam on Hess Creek northeast of Livengood to provide water for a dredging operation. It also began excavating a 3,200-foot tunnel from Hess Creek to the head of Livengood Creek.

Later that year the Interstate-Callahan Company acquired a 75 percent interest in Livengood Placers and advanced funds to continue work on the dam and tunnel, as well as build support facilities such as the warehouse.

Unfortunately, unsteady economic conditions during the 1930s brought little investment into the company. Consequently, work on the fledgling project ground to a halt. In 1939, Livengood Placers finally received a $1,050,000 loan from the federal government's Reconstruction Finance Corporation (RFC) and resumed work on the project.

While work was being completed on the water supply, along with ground thawing and stripping, a diesel-powered Yuba gold dredge, with six-cubic-foot buckets, was trucked in and assembled. It began operations in October 1940 and operated through 1941 with less-than-anticipated yields. The company was forced to borrow additional funds to cover construction costs, and ended up owing the RFC $1,500,000.00.

Unfortunately, in 1942 the federal government shut down all gold-mining activities across the nation for the duration of World War II. According to Audrey Parker's book, *Livengood, the Last Stampede*, the dredge did not start up again until 1946.

Livengood Placers operated the dredge through the summer of 1954, but was never able to dig itself out of debt.

Even before the dredge resumed operations after World War II the RFC had urged the FE Co. to take over Livengood Placers, but FE Co. officials declined. According to Spence's book, the RFC threatened foreclosure, and in late 1954 followed through on that threat.

The RFC put Livengood Placer's assets up for sale, and the FE Co. bought the dredge and extra parts, thawing and stripping equipment, and machine shop equipment for $150,000. The FE Co. wasn't interested in the Livengood claims.

The dredge, with its on-board diesel power plant, was designed for remote operations. According to John Boswell's history of the FE Co., the dredge was disassembled and trucked to Fairbanks where its pontoons were re-assembled in the Chena River to use as a barge.

Laden with supplies, the pontoon/barge was then pushed 750 miles down the Chena, Tanana and Yukon Rivers; and up the Koyukuk River to the Hogatza "Hog" River. At Hog Landing it was disassembled, and everything trucked 26 miles to Bear Creek. After reassembly, it started dredging in 1957. After successfully operating for many years, it now sits amidst Bear Creek's dredge tailings.

The Livengood warehouse is on private property. Before exploring the area please check out land status and get permission from land owners.

Sources

- Conversation with Karl Hanneman, Fairbanks resident with experience mining in Livengood area. 2016
- *History of Operations of United States Smelting, Refining and Mining Company.* John Boswell. Mineral Industries Research Laboratory, University of Alaska. 1979
- *Livengood, the Last Stampede.* Audrey Parker. Hats Off Books. 2003
- *The Northern Gold Fleet, Twentieth-Century Gold Dredging in Alaska.* Clark Spence. University of Illinois Press 1996

Manley schoolhouse in mid-2000s

Manley's historic schoolhouse reflects town's commitment to education

Gladys Dart was a young mother with three children when she moved to Manley Hot Springs in 1956. She and her husband, Chuck, had just purchased the Karshner homestead on the north side of Hot Springs Slough and were in the process of starting a greenhouse operation.

Manley Hot Springs, now usually just called Manley, was past its zenith when the Darts moved there. John Karshner had staked his homestead around the hot springs in 1902, and a community coalesced there. According to U.S. Census reports, Manley's 1910 population was 101. However, it had shrunk to 29 residents by 1920. The population swelled to 45 by 1930, but slipped back down to 29 by 1950.

Gladys wrote in a 1983 biography that 15 people lived in Manley during the winter of 1956-57, mostly "old timers and childless couples." The Northern Commercial Company's store manager had a teenage daughter, and there was only one other family with children.

The territorial government's policy was that communities needed 10 students before a teacher was provided. It is doubtful that until the 1950s Manley had enough children to warrant a school, except perhaps during its earliest boom years.

Because of this, Manley parents with school-age children faced difficult choices. They could move their families to communities with schools, board their children away from home, or teach them through correspondence.

The Darts home-schooled their oldest child that year. The next year a family with school-age children moved back to Manley. The father was a local bush pilot, but his wife and children lived in Fairbanks. The family's desire to be together brought them all back to Manley.

Gladys told me that even though she had taught school in Fairbanks, teaching again in a formal school setting was not in their plans. However, a few Manley residents, convinced that more families would move to town if there was a school, approached Gladys about starting a school.

In addition to the 10-student minimum, communities also needed to provide a school building, so the Darts offered the use of an old 16' by 20' log cabin on their property. The building had no electricity or plumbing, but it did have hot water piped from the springs for heat.

The Territory accepted the one-room schoolhouse. Gladys became the school's sole teacher, and Chuck provided the maintenance. However, by the start of school in September 1958 the schoolhouse still didn't have furniture or supplies. Manley was not yet connected to Fairbanks by road, and the supplies would be delivered by the last boat of the season, due about a month after school started.

Until the furniture arrived, they had to make do. Chuck shortened the legs of two large tables to serve as desks, and students used Blazo boxes (wooden crates that 5-gallon tins of fuel were shipped in) as seats.

Gladys survived that first school year, and predictions about the school attracting new residents proved true. By 1960 Manley had 72 residents, and the school had 19 students — a bit crowded for a one-room building.

Classes moved out of the log schoolhouse in fall 1961 and shared space temporarily in the Dart's newly finished home. A new school building was completed in 1963. That building served until 1980 when an even larger facility (named after Gladys) was constructed.

The log schoolhouse (which is on private property) was renovated for its 50th anniversary in 2008 and is still nestled against the base of the hill, just off the Elliott Highway. It is a testament to the tenacity of a lady and a community that valued education. Gladys died in 2019 and is buried in Manley.

Sources:

- *Chuck and Gladys Dart: Manley Hot Springs*. Chuck and Gladys Dart. Yukon-Koyukuk School District. 1983
- Conversation with Gladys Dart. 2015
- *In deed, indeed: teaching and learning in a one-room school*. Gladys Dart. Outskirts Press. 2010
- U.S. Census reports for 1910 through 1960

1929 Caterpillar tractor recently restored by Jim Gibertoni. The Cat spent most of its life in Manley.

An old Manley tractor still putters along

In 1929, C.W. Cash, a sales representative for Northern Commercial Company, traveled through Interior Alaska visiting prospective customers. While in Manley he met with Jim Liska, who had been running freight in the Manley area for years using horse-drawn wagons and sleds.

After test driving a small Caterpillar tractor, Liska decided to purchase a Caterpillar Fifteen, also referred to as a Cat-15. The Cat-15 was a small gasoline-powered tracked tractor, putting out 15 horsepower. It normally came with a 40-inch wide track, but could also be ordered with a 50-

inch track which made the tractor wider than it was tall and more stable on slopes. The tractor had three forward and one reverse gear, and a top speed of about 9 mph. It weighed 5,790 pounds and could pull its own weight.

Liska ordered the Cat-15 with a 50" track, and snow and ice grousers (cleats that attached to the track to increase traction). The tractor arrived in Fairbanks via the Alaska Railroad in 1930, and by November 1930 Liska was hauling freight from Manley to Eureka, about 25 miles.

Liska also ran freight between Fairbanks and Manley using his new Cat. At that time there was no all-season road to Manley. An all-season road had been blazed from Fairbanks to Livengood in 1928, but a road from Livengood to Manley was not completed until 1958.

The only viable land-route was the old Washington-Alaska Military Cable and Telegraph System (WAMCATS) sled road which followed the Tanana River from Manley to Dunbar, a section camp for the Alaska Railroad (ARR). From Dunbar, the sled road paralleled the railroad tracks to Fairbanks. The WAMCATS route traversed several marshy areas, so it was unusable during the summer.

According to Claus-M. Naske's book, *Paving Alaska's Trails*, Manley-area residents had lobbied the Alaska Road Commission (ARC) for years to build an all-season road. However, with reliable summer riverboats plying the Tanana, the ARC never acquiesced. The all-season road from Livengood to Manley was not completed until after the ARR ceased riverboat service along the Tanana River.

Liska used the 80-mile WAMCATS route for winter freighting. The trip took 20 hours travel-time one-way, with tractor-plus-sleds making about 4 mph. The Cat's 23-gallon tank was too small to hold enough fuel for the entire trip, so refueling along the way was necessary. Liska carried extra fuel, but Jim Gibertoni, the tractor's current owner, told me that Liska probably also cached fuel along the route at communities like Old Minto and Tolovana, where fuel could be dropped off by riverboat during the summer.

Gibertoni also related to me that Liska did not immediately abandon his horses after buying the Cat-15. Early tractors were notoriously hard to extricate once stuck, so two horses accompanied the tractor-train to help pull it out of trouble.

In addition to freighting, Liska used the tractor for grading roads in the Manley area, as well as hauling wood. It was also utilized in Manley for a variety of other functions. With a belt attached to the power-take-off at the rear of the tractor, it alternately powered water pumps, a small sawmill, and a DC dynamo which provided electricity to much of Manley.

Liska died in 1948. After his death the Cat went through a series of owners, always staying in the Manley area until Gibertoni purchased it from Cy Hetherington. Gibertoni, who lives in Fairbanks and recently retired, was looking for a tractor to restore when the Cat became available.

Gibertoni brought the still functional tractor to Fairbanks, and completely disassembled and rebuilt it, having new parts manufactured when necessary.

The almost-all-original-equipment Cat-15 was displayed NC Machinery on Van Horn Road for several years, but is now in storage, awaiting a more permanent venue for viewing.

Sources:

- Conversation with Jim Gibertoni, current owner of the Manley Caterpillar Fifteen tractor
- "Paving Alaska's Trails, The Work of the Alaska Road Commission." Claus-M. Naske. University Press of America. 1986
- *Standard Catalog of Farm Tractors, 1890 – 1980."* C. H. Wendel. Krause Publications. 2000
- *"Stanley Dayo, Manley Hot Springs – A Biography."* Yukon-Koyukuk School District. Spirit Mountain Press. 1985

Steese Highway - Fox

The LeTourneau "Sno-Freighter" ias it looks today sitting along the Stese Highway in Fox.

LeTourneau Sno-freighter made Arctic transportation history

On a hillside along the Steese Highway south of Fox, sits a relic of the Cold War, a "sno-freighter" used in the mid-1950s to move supplies from Central Alaska to the Arctic coast for construction of the Distant Early Warning (DEW) Line. The DEW Line was a series of military radar stations (no longer in existence) arrayed in a 6,000-mile arc across Northern Alaska, Canada and Greenland.

The sno-freighter is a "land train" built by R.G. LeTourneau Inc. These land trains, developed as off-road vehicles, were (in train fashion) multiple wheeled cars linked together. Their motive power was individual electric motors located in the hub of each wheel. This arrangement evenly distributed power across all the wheels, providing better traction.

LeTourneau worked on development of land trains until the first heavy lift helicopters went into production in 1962. These helicopters eliminated much of the land-train market.

Between 1953 and 1962 the company developed five land trains, each one unique. The VC-22 Sno-Freighter (shown in the drawing) is the second one LeTourneau produced. It was built for Alaska Freight Lines, owned by Al Ghezzi. Ghezzi was a pioneering Alaska trucker — his company was the first to keep Thompson Pass north of Valdez open in the winter.

General Electric Corporation (GE) was the main contractor for DEW Line construction, and Ghezzi obtained a contract from GE to deliver 500 tons of freight to the Canadian Arctic. The sno-freighter was a key part of his plans for the supply effort.

The vehicle has a lead power unit, plus five trailers. The lead unit is 16' wide and about 45' long. It contained a control section, a bunk section for its four-man crew, and a power section. Power for the train was provided by two 400 hp Cummins diesel generators. The generators provided electricity for the vehicle's controls, and to run the electric motors that drove the sno-freighter's 24 wheels. (The power section is now gone.)

Each trailer is 16' wide and 40' long. The complete land-train is 274' long, and towers above the ground on 88"-high balloon tires.

According to the book, *LeTourneau Earthmovers,* in February 1955 the sno-freighter was shipped disassembled from LeTourneau's Texas plant to Circle, located at the end of the Steese Highway about 135 miles northeast of Fairbanks. LeTourneau technicians accompanied the land train and re-assembled it at Circle.

A 1950s LeTourneau brochure touts the land-train's off-road capability. However, the same brochure says that it was designed to utilize 'bulldozed trails" in heavily-vegetated areas. Indeed, when the sno-freighter (carrying 150 tons of cargo) left Circle headed northeast towards the Canadian Arctic, it was accompanied by five bulldozers to blaze a trail, and 32 Mack trucks with loaded trailers. (With 500 tons to be delivered, Ghezzi needed more than just the sno-freighter to fulfill his contract.)

The land train worked well during its first winter trek. The caravan covered about 1,000 miles round-trip, returning in the spring to Eagle where the sno-freighter was parked for the summer. (Eagle, located about 300 miles east of Fairbanks, is the northern terminus of the Taylor Highway.)

Resupplied for the next winter freighting caravan, the sno-freighter made it into Canada before an accidental fire destroyed its generators. Without power, and with no possibility of immediate repair, the land train was abandoned, while the rest of the caravan moved on.

Cliff Bishop, in his book, *Eighteen Wheels North to Alaska*, wrote that the sno-freighter was eventually towed back to Boundary, just inside the U.S. border. Bishop participated in the recovery and moving of the land train, car by car, from Boundary to Tok. Its final destination was Fairbanks.

The sno-freighter was eventually bought by long-time Fairbanks resident Bobby Miller, and was later acquired by Rick Winther, who also has deep Fairbanks ties. Rick originally hoped to display the land train at Pioneer Park, but when those plans fell through. John Reeves allowed him to store the sno-freighter on Reeves' Fox property. Anyone traveling the Steese Highway can now view this piece of Cold War transportation history.

Sources:
- "Conversation with Rick Winther, owner of the LeTourneau sno-freighter
- *Eighteen Wheels North to Alaska – a History of Trucking in Alaska*. Cliff Bishop. Publication Consultants. 2009
- *LeTourneau Earthmovers*. Eric C. Orlemann. MBI. 2001
- "New Horizons in Off-Road Transportation." R. G. LeTourneau, Inc... No date (c 1955)
- "Trucks Blaze New Winter Trails Northeast to the Arctic." In *Fairbanks Daily News-Miner*. Nov. 8, 1955

Steese Highway - Fairbanks Creek

Hi-Yu was one of Fairbanks area's most successful hard-rock gold mines

The Hi-Yu mine as it looked in the 1990s

About 25 miles northeast of Fairbanks sits one of the area's most successful lode mines, now abandoned and decaying. The Hi-Yu Mine, the second-largest lode mine in the Fairbanks area during the first half of the 1900s, produced 110,000 ounces of gold.

The Hi-Yu is located in the Fairbanks Creek valley, which was one of the richest gold-producing areas in the Fairbanks Mining District. Mining activity along the creek represented all the major forms of gold recovery used during the early 20th century: open-cut mining, drifting, dredging, and hard-rock (lode).

In 1912 Clarence Crites and Harry Feldman discovered the lode claim, a rich gold-bearing quartz vein on Moose Creek, about a half-mile upstream from its confluence with Fairbanks Creek. It was one of the last significant lode discoveries during that time period.

According to a 2002 article by Curtis Freeman in *Alaska Miner* magazine, Crites and Feldman were looking for new lode-gold prospects in the Fairbanks area, and two local Athabascan residents informed them of a likely site on Moose Creek. The mine's name, "Hi-Yu," is supposedly an approximation of the Athabascan words for "white rocks," referring to the gold-bearing quartz found at the site.

The book, *Historic Resources in the Fairbanks North Star Borough*, states that the two partners quickly built a cabin and sank several prospecting shafts (what we called "coyote holes" in California). By the next year they had begun tunneling into the hillside.

In 1914, the mine was in full production, and Crites and Feldman moved a five-stamp mill from Chatham Creek (on the opposite side of the ridge) to the Hi-Yu site to process their ore. The stamp mill, which had a capacity of processing 15 tons of ore every 24 hours, crushed the ore with heavy, vertical pistons called stamps, allowing the gold to be removed.

By 1930, the partners had acquired several new claims adjacent to the mine site and erected a building to house the stamp mill equipment. They also added an assay office the same year. Four years later they built a larger-capacity five-stamp mill on the site of the old mill.

In 1934, a mess hall was constructed on the hillside above the mill, and a 30-man bunkhouse was added a year later. The millhouse was expanded in 1936 with the construction of a new power plant, office, and the addition of five more stamps (10 total), doubling the mill's capacity.

By this time miners had blasted four main tunnels into the hillside, and a small railway system was installed to transport ore from tunnel to mill.

By 1941, the millhouse had again been enlarged to include a garage and a sauna for the workers. Several ancillary buildings such as coal storage shed an explosives cabin had been added, and two residences for the mine superintendent and engineers had been constructed.

Unfortunately, the advent of World War II forced the closure of the Hi-Yu mine, as well as almost every other gold mine in the United States. In 1942, under War Production Board Limitation Order No. 208, the federal government closed gold mining as a non-essential war-time activity.

The Hi-Yu, like many mines, never re-opened. Low gold prices and increased production costs made re-opening the mine uneconomical. Except for a few brief periods of activity, most of the facilities have sat abandoned and deteriorating for over 50 years.

The bunkhouse burned in 1969. The 3 ½ story wood-frame millhouse is still in remarkably good condition. However, it is considered dangerous, and has been enclosed by a chain-link fence to deter the curious.

The site is now owned by the state of Alaska Mental Health Trust Authority.

Sources:

- Fairbanks North Star Borough property records
- *Historic Resources in the Fairbanks North Star Borough*. Janet Matheson & F. Bruce Haldeman. Fairbanks North Star Borough. 1981
- "History of lode mining, Fairbanks district." Curtis Freeman. In *Alaska Miner* magazine, Vol. 30, No. 8, August 2002
- "Hi-Yu; Crites and Feldman Mine." From the Mine-Dat.org website, an outreach project of the Hudson Institute of Mineralogy. 2015
- *Lode Deposits of the Fairbanks District*, Alaska. James M. Hill. U.S.G.S. Bulletin 849-B.1933

North side of blacksmith shop at Fairbanks Creek Camp in early spring of 1994

Fairbanks Creek Camp was one of F.E. Co.'s final ventures in Fairbanks area

Gold Dredge No. 2, located about 20 miles northeast of Fairbanks at Fairbanks Creek, was one of Fairbanks Exploration Company's (F.E. Company) last operational dredges. The dredge was constructed on Lower Goldstream Creek in 1927-28, but was moved to Fairbanks Creek in 1949.

The move was accomplished during winter. A trail between Goldstream and Fairbanks Creeks was cleared in early winter, and snow allowed to accumulate. Dredge No. 2 was disassembled and in March was moved in sections with each section positioned on sled tracks and towed by four D-8 tractors.

In his book on the history of the F.E. Company, John Boswell stated that the dredge's weight plus the friction from the sled runners melted snow under the runners so they actually ran on a thin layer of water. This eased transport, but when the tractors stopped, the runners immediately froze to the ground. This problem was remedied by laying spruce and cottonwood poles crosswise across the road (called "corduroy") underneath the runners. This necessitated either advance planning for stops, or jacking the dredge section up to put the corduroy under the runners.

The move was completed on schedule and the dredge re-assembled and put into operation. Except for one incident, Dredge No. 2 labored uninterrupted (taking into account winter shut-down, of course) until 1963, when the F.E. Company shut it down permanently.

The incident that marred the dredge's career was its accidental sinking in April 1959. The accident occurred when a deckhand tried to dislodge a chuck of ice from the stacker (the long tunnel-like apparatus at the back of the dredge used to discharge rocks and gravel). Instead of breaking up the ice with a pike pole, he used a stick of dynamite and ended up sending the dredge to the bottom of the pond. The dredge pond had to be drained and the dredge repaired and re-floated, which wasn't completed until September 1959.

Fairbanks Creek Camp was constructed to support F.E. Company's dredging operations, which included exploratory work, clearing and thawing of ground, and the dredging itself. According to the book, *Historic Resources in the Fairbanks North Star Borough*, the camp originally included 12 buildings: several small single-story bunkhouses, a laundry, two-story combination bunkhouse and mess hall, food cache, cook's residence, blacksmith's shop, garage, and sheds.

All of the buildings at Fairbanks Creek Camp were of wood-frame construction. Their construction and appearance were similar to other F.E. Company support camps like those at Ester and Chatanika.

Many of the camp's buildings were sheathed with metal siding. Most had floor joists covered with planks, and sat on wood timbers so they could be easily moved. (In fact, many of the buildings had been moved from the Lower Goldstream area.) The blacksmith shop and garage, however, had dirt floors.

The drawing shows one of the outside walls of the blacksmith shop, and the turnbuckles and other items stored there. The camp smithy fabricated or repaired many of the simpler implements used in dredging operations.

More complicated items (anything requiring machining or with intricate parts) were worked on at the F.E. Company machine shop in Fairbanks. It's hard to envision what some of the metal pieces we found stored at F.E. Company shops were used for, however, one of those strange pieces now supports our mailbox.

When I visited the camp in the early 1990s, the buildings had been sitting empty for 30 years. A few of them had already collapsed.

John Reeves bought the property in the late 1990s, and as part of the sale he was required to remove most of the camp buildings, which were on un-patented mining claims.

Many of the buildings went to Gold Dredge No. 8, but the two-story bunkhouse/mess hall was hauled to Cleary Summit and is now the Mount Aurora Lodge. The few buildings left at Fairbanks Creek Camp are on private property and the access road is gated.

Sources:

- Conversation with John Reeves, owner of Fairbanks Creek property
- *Historic Resources in the Fairbanks North Star Borough*. Janet Matheson & F. Bruce Haldeman. Fairbanks North Star Borough. 1981
- *History of Alaskan Operations of Unites States Smelting, Refining and Mining Company*. John C. Boswell. Mineral Industries Research Laboratory, University of Alaska. 1979
- *The Northern Gold Fleet: Twentieth-Century Gold Dredging in Alaska*. Clark C. Spence. University of Illinois Press. 1996

Chatanika Gold Camp as it looked in 1994

Old FE Company camp still an important part of Chatanika

On a southeast-facing hill just north of Mile 27.5 of the Steese Highway sits Chatanika Gold Camp. The camp used to be the Fairbanks Exploration Company's (FE. Co.) operations base for gold dredging along Cleary Creek.

Cleary Creek is an eight-mile-long stream running northwesterly from Cleary Summit to the Chatanika River. It was one of the richest gold-bearing streams around Fairbanks and supported two mining camps. The town of Chatanika was near the creek's mouth, and Cleary City sat a few miles to the northeast.

The first mines in the area were drift mines that began petering out in the 1910s when higher-concentration placer-gold deposits were exhausted.

However, after the Alaska Railroad was completed in 1923 and heavy equipment could be freighted to Fairbanks, the FE Co. moved into the area. The company began buying placer claims and doing preparatory work for bringing in gold dredges, which could take advantage of what was left in the area — large, low-grade, placer-gold deposits.

One of the first areas developed by the FE Co. was the Cleary Creek drainage. Between 1923 and 1925 it built an operations camp about half-way between Chatanika and Cleary City.

According to National Register of Historic Places documents, the camp at Chatanika was the largest one the FE Co. had in the Fairbanks area. This is understandable since two dredges churned the Cleary Creek gravels.

Gold Dredge No. 3 began operations at the old Chatanika townsite in 1928. That was the same year that the Davidson Ditch, which channeled water from the upper Chatanika River for dredging operations, was completed. Dredge No. 3 still sits about a mile west of the camp, across the highway from Chatanika Lodge.

Dredge No. 5 was put into service a year later to take advantage of placer-gold deposits along upper Cleary Creek. Except for a brief period during World War II when all the area dredges were idled, that dredge worked Cleary Creek until 1947, when it was moved to Little Eldorado Creek and later to Dome Creek.

Dredge No. 3 continued to operate until 1963 when, due to increasing operating costs and low gold prices, it shut down. The camp remained dormant until being sold in 1976 to Robert Galeoto and his wife, who developed the property into a resort, converting one of the buildings into a restaurant.

In 1979 the camp was added to the National Register of Historic places. There were 12 buildings included in the listing. Six of the buildings, including the camp's office, were small wood-framed and wood-sided structures that were perhaps built before the FE Co. moved into the area.

Five of the structures were built by the FE Co. in 1925. All those buildings were wood-frame structures covered with corrugated metal siding and having corrugated metal roofs.

The largest of those metal-sided buildings are a 36-man bunkhouse/mess hall and a 52-man bunkhouse. Both of those buildings are two-stories high.

The bunkhouse/mess hall building (which is the restaurant) is a 36' by 72' structure with gabled roof. (The mess hall still contains its original eight-foot-long wood-burning cookstove and most of the original furnishings.) The 52-man bunkhouse is 31' by 60' with a 16' by 26' addition to the northeast. Both the 52-man bunkhouse and addition have hipped roofs. Other metal-sided camp buildings include the blacksmith shop, the boiler house, and the garage.

The drawing shows the 52-man bunkhouse in the foreground, with the bunkhouse/mess hall and garage in the background. The view is looking west towards the old Chatanika townsite and Gold Dredge No. 3.

That's the Old Steese Highway running in front of the buildings. The remains of the Davidson Ditch snake along the hillside above the camp, and the old Chatanika schoolhouse (now a small museum) is about a ¼ mile to the northwest.

The camp is now owned by Marlene and Matt Bach, and Val and Red Scullion. Marlene and Val's father, Otto Babenicek, once operated the Chatanika trading post (now the Chatanika Lodge). Marlene told me her father also cooked at the FE Co. camp in 1949. How fitting that a family with connections to the FE Company's Chatanika operations now runs the camp.

Sources:

- "Chatanika Gold Camp National Register of Historic Places Inventory-Nomination Form." John S. Kaufman. National Park Service. 1979
- Conversation with Marlene Bach, one of the camp's owners
- Fairbanks North Star Borough property records
- *History of Alaskan Operations of United States Smelting, Refining and Mining Company.* John C. Boswell. Mineral Industries Research Laboratory, University of Alaska. 1979

Steese Highway - Chatanika

Old Chatanika cabin in 1994

The changing fortunes of Old Chatanika

In 1902 Felix Pedro washed gold out of Cleary Creek about 25 miles northeast of Fairbanks. Few miners worked the creeks near Fairbanks in 1902. Not until the end of the next summer were there any big strikes. Cleary Creek then became one of the richest gold-producing areas near Fairbanks, and by 1904 two camps had sprung up along the eight-mile-long stream.

Cleary City was established along the upper creek. Another camp, which, according to Nicholas Deely's book, *Tanana Valley Railroad, the Gold Dust Line*, was called 15 Below-Cleary (the 15th claim below the creek's discovery claim), coalesced farther down the creek near the Chatanika River. The lower camp was eventually re-named Chatanika.

In 1907 Chatanika became the northern terminus for the Tanana Valley Railroad (TVRR). Chatanika's achievement was the result of fortuitous circumstances rather than deliberate planning, though. The TVRR reached Gilmore, just a few miles northeast of Fox, in 1905. Builders planned to extend the line over Cleary Summit ridge to reach the rich diggings at Fairbanks Creek and in the Upper Cleary Creek drainage near Cleary City.

However, new mines were opening to the northwest of Gilmore, in the Dome and Vault Creek areas (in the valleys on either side of the present-day Elliott Highway about 15 miles north of Fairbanks).

This new development prompted the TVRR to change routes. Instead of continuing in a northeasterly direction over the ridge towards Cleary Creek, the route doubled back and climbed Fox Gulch before crossing into the Chatanika River drainage.

Tracks reached Chatanika in September 1907 but were never extended beyond to Cleary City. Chatanika became the trans-shipment point for people and supplies headed to Cleary City and other destinations. Chatanika's position was further bolstered when, in November 1907, the business district of Cleary City burned down and about half that city's residents moved to Chatanika.

Chatanika began as a tent camp, but soon progressed to log cabin town. Early photographs show a business district comprised of wood-frame buildings, many with false-fronts. The rest of the community was primarily small wood-frame houses and log cabins, with log cabins predominating.

The town's glory days were short-lived. At its zenith Chatanika probably boasted about 500 residents. Gold production from drift mining peaked in 1909 as easily mined deposits were exhausted, and the town's population began dwindling. The *Dictionary of Alaska Place Names* records that by 1930 only 30 people called Chatanika home.

The introduction of gold dredges along Cleary Creek sealed Chatanika's fate. The Fairbanks Exploration Company (FE Co.) began buying up Cleary Creek claims in the 1920s, built a support camp (Chatanika Gold Camp) in 1923-25, and started dredging Lower Cleary Creek in 1928 and Upper Cleary in 1929.

Unfortunately, the town of Chatanika sat atop claims that the FE Co. planned to develop. After the TVRR shut down in 1930 most of the town was torn up so that Dredge No. 3 (still sitting at Chatanika) could expand operations.

The southern edge of Chatanika, above the limits of dredging, was spared. When I hiked into the abandoned settlement in the mid 1990s only a few structures remained. The building pictured in the drawing is one survivor. (Recent aerial photos indicate that it is still there.) It is a metal-roofed log cabin with a wood-frame porch tacked on to the front. The porch is sheathed with white-washed ship-lap siding, but vertical rough-sawn planking covers the log portion of the cabin. The book, *Historic Resources in the Fairbanks North Star Borough*, states that the log-cabin portion of the structure probably dates from around 1910.

In addition to extant cabins and several collapsed buildings, numerous implements such as a rusted wheel barrow, tin-lined storage box, and an old donkey engine used to lie scattered about. The remains of what is now called "Old Chatanika" are on private property. Please respect private property owner's rights if you plan to explore the Chatanika area.

Sources:

- *Dictionary of Alaska Place Names*. Donald J. Orth. U.S. Geological Survey. 1971
- *History of Alaskan Operations of United States Smelting, Refining and Mining Company*. John Boswell. Mineral Industries Research Library, University of Alaska. 1979
- *Historic Resources in the Fairbanks North Star Borough*. Janet Matheson & F. Bruce Haldeman. Fairbanks North Star Borough. 1981
- *Steamboats on the Chena*. Basil Hendricks & Susan Savage. Epicenter Press. 1988
- *Tanana Valley Railroad*, the Gold Dust Line. Nicholas Deely. Denali Designs. 1996

Steese Highway - Chatanika

Entrance to Poker Flat Research Range launch facility, just past Chatanika, along the Steese Highway

The origins of Poker Flat Research Range

Poker Flat Research Range, owned and operated by the University of Alaska's Geophysical Institute (GI), is a rocket range located at Chatanika, 30 miles north of Fairbanks. Construction on the facility began in 1968, but the site's development was years in the making.

In the 1950s scientists across the United States and Canada began using sounding rockets for meteorological testing, and in 1959 the Meteorological Rocket Network (MRN) was formed to foster synoptic weather observations. One of the launch sites for the MRN was at Fort Greely near Delta Junction.

According to Neil Davis's book, *Rockets over Alaska*, scientists from the University of Alaska's GI participated in Fort Greely rocket launches in 1964 to study noctilucent clouds. Also, Fort Wainwright had a small missile testing facility, and GI personnel participated in launches there in 1965 for auroral studies.

Neither of the two sites were ideal for launching scientific rockets, and GI personnel became convinced that Alaska needed its own launch facility. Neil Davis, who graduated from the University of Alaska in 1961 with a Ph.D. in physics and eventually became the GI's assistant director, was instrumental in establishing Poke Flat Research Range.

An Alaska launch site needed to be located where ground observations could be conducted during a rocket's flight. Davis found an ideal site just past Chatanika. The area was sparsely populated, as were lands to the north all the way to the Arctic Ocean. The site also lay along a line between the GI's primary aurora viewing stations at Ester Dome and Fort Yukon. Observations could also be done from Barter Island, father north.

The site was accessible via the Steese Highway, a White Alice communications site at nearby Pedro Dome could be linked to, and electrical power was readily available.

Davis secured a long-term lease on 5,132 acres of land at Chatanika from the Fairbanks North Star Borough. The U.S. Interior Department also agreed that federal lands farther north could be utilized for rocket landings.

By 1966 the Poker Flat launch facility existed on paper. All that was lacking were funds to build it. Those funds were not immediately forthcoming, which meant that GI scientists needing to launch rockets had to use a rocket range at Fort Churchill in Manitoba, Canada.

That changed with the January 1968 crash of a U.S. B52 bomber in Greenland. The U.S. had military facilities in Greenland, and the bomber, which was carrying thermonuclear bombs, crashed while attempting an emergency landing at Thule Air Base.

Because of the incident, the Danish government (Greenland is part of the Kingdom of Denmark) curtailed most U.S. military operations in Greenland. This was disastrous for the U.S. military, but fortuitous for Alaska.

At that time the U.S. Defense Department (DOD) was developing a series of rocket-boosted experiments aimed at developing the capability to detect atmospheric nuclear weapons testing by the Soviet Union.

Launches had been planned for a rocket range in Greenland, but with Greenland now off-limits, another launch facility near the arctic had to be used. Fort Churchill was booked up, so it was agreed that the launches be moved to the as-yet unbuilt Fairbanks range.

With limited funds from the U.S. government and lots of Northern ingenuity, Davis and his crews began work on the Poker Flat facility in July 1968. A rudimentary facility was operational by the beginning of March 1969, and during that month six military sounding rockets were successfully launched, also inaugurating Poker Flat operations.

According to a GI history of the rocket range, the DOD wanted to close the range after completing its launches. Davis convinced it to keep the range open by agreeing to provide the necessary ground-based observations for the DOD launches only if the university could launch its own NASA-sponsored rocket afterwards.

The DOD agreed and the NASA-sponsored rocket became the first launch by a civilian agency from the range. Poker Flat limped along on a meagerly budget for several years after that while proving that it was dependable and provided a useful location for scientific experiments.

The Poker Flat Research Range, the only university-owned rocket range in the world, is still in operation. Now much expanded, it has launched more than 2,000 rockets in the past 50 years.

Sources:

- "A brief history of Poker Flat." On UAF *Geophysical Institute Poker Flat Research Range* webpage. No date
- "Cold War inspired the first launch from Poker Flat" Ned Rozell. In *Fairbanks Daily News-Miner*. 2-18-2017
- "Neal Brown gives a lecture entitled 'History and stories about Poker Flats research' on September 25, 2017 in the Schaible Auditorium at the University of Alaska in Fairbanks, Alaska." Neal Brown. University of Alaska, Fairbanks Oral History Collection. 2017
- *Rockets over Alaska: The Genesis of Poker Flat*. Neil Davis. Alaska-Yukon Press. 2006

Steese Highway - Eagle Creek

Berry Camp along Eagle Creek, at about Mile 103 of the Steese Highway, just south of Eagle Summit

Clarence Berry had major impact on Interior Alaska mining

Clarence Berry was one of the "Kings of the Klondike," that small cohort of early gold-seekers who made fortunes in the diggings around Dawson City in the Yukon Territory.

Born in 1867, Clarence grew up near Fresno, California and by 1893 was operating a fruit farm. However, the depression of the 1890s forced him to abandon his fields. Eager for fresh opportunities, he headed to Alaska in 1894 with friends.

The group landed at Dyea, hiked over Chilkoot Pass, and eventually reached the diggings along the Fortymile River. Clarence ended up mining at Franklin Creek, a tributary of the Fortymile where gold had been discovered in 1886.

In the fall of 1895 he returned to California, and married his childhood sweetheart, Ethel Bush, in March of 1896. The day after the wedding, with little money but high hopes, Clarence, Ethel, and Clarence's youngest brother, Fred, took off for the Yukon.

Settling back into the Fortymile country, Clarence was unsuccessful at prospecting. He ended up bartending at Bill McPhee's saloon in Forty Mile, the community at the confluence of the Fortymile and Yukon Rivers that served as the region's administrative center.

George Carmack, who was one of the first men to discover gold in the Klondike, had to register his claims at Forty Mile, and Clarence was behind the counter when Carmack came into the saloon to announce his good fortune. Encouraged by Ethel, Clarence and Fred immediately set off up-river to stake a claim.

Their claim, along with others they acquired interests in, proved rich. According to a 2013 article by Michael Gates in the *Yukon News*, when Clarence and Ethel arrived in Seattle on the S.S. Portland in July of 1897 they carried $130,000 in gold with them—$9 million at today's gold price.

Clarence used some of his profits to become one of the first miners in the Klondike to invest in steam equipment to improve efficiency. After noticing that steam exhaust from his boiler was thawing the ground, he ingeniously channeled the exhaust into a rubber hose and through a rifle barrel rammed into the frozen ground, consequently being credited as the first to use steam to thaw frozen ground. He was also the first to install electric lights at his mines.

When the placer gold deposits supporting the Berrys' mines began petering out, they moved operations to Ester Creek west of Fairbanks. Matthew Reckard, in a 1999 article in *The Ester Republic*, states that the mining camp of Berry, where the Berry family made another fortune, was located a couple of miles down Ester Creek from the camp at Ester.

From Ester, the Berrys moved on to the Circle Mining District in about 1909. Oscar Bredlie, who carried mail between Chatanika and Circle, told Jane Williams in a 1983 interview that the Berrys' first venture in that area was at Berry Camp, on Eagle Creek south of Eagle Summit.

Berry Camp, which can be seen below the Steese Highway as you climb Eagle Summit, is shown in the drawing. The camp, which is on the south side of Eagle Creek, was the support camp for a hydraulic mining operation. The two lines of vegetation seen at the top of the drawing mark the remains of ditches excavated to carry water from Upper Eagle Creek to mining areas lower down the creek.

The camp was located along the old winter trail over Eagle Summit. Although never billed as a roadhouse, it was a frequent stopping place for travelers, and evidently supported a lively little community. During construction of the Steese highway in the late 1920s it was utilized as a road construction camp.

The Berrys also mined over the divide along Mammoth Creek where they successfully operated a dredge for many years. Clarence, who eventually resettled to California with Ethel, died in 1930.

Berry Camp is located on private property. Please check land status and get property owners' permission before exploring the area.

Sources:

- "Berry, the Post Office on Ester Creek." Matthew Reckard. In *The Ester Republic*. Vol. 1 No. 10, October 1999
- *Dictionary of Alaska Place Names, Geological Survey professional paper 567*. Donald J. Orth. U.S. Geological Survey. 1971
- "The Horatio Alger Story of Clarence Berry." Michael Gates. In *Yukon News*. 5-3-2013

Circle Hot Springs Road - Cemetery Road

Deadwood Cemetery in 2017

Deadwood Cemetery burials tell the history of Central area

Turning on to Circle Hot Springs Road at Central and driving about 3/4 mile, you come to Cemetery Road just before crossing Graveyard Creek. About 1/2 mile along Cemetery Road lies a small burial ground. Only about a quarter-acre in size, the cemetery holds 36 graves, the oldest dating to 1905.

Established before Circle Hot Springs Road was built, the cemetery was originally situated next to the four-mile trail (blazed in the late 1890s) linking Central and Deadwood Creek. Now called Central Cemetery, early residents referred to it as Deadwood Cemetery.

Ruth Olson, a long-time area resident who spent her early childhood on Deadwood Creek, related in a 1997 interview with Jane Williams that during Circle Mining District's early years there was little at Central besides a roadhouse.

Aside from a small Athabaskan enclave at Medicine Lake (just north of Circle Hot Springs), most people in the Central-Circle Hot Springs area were gold miners living along nearby creeks — primarily Deadwood Creek.

A 1905 U.S.G.S report states that in 1903 there were about 35 miners operating along Deadwood Creek and its tributaries. Between 1906 and 1924 Deadwood Creek had the only post office within 20 miles. Mammoth Creek to the west also had a post office. Central did not gain its post office until after Deadwood Creek's postmaster died.

Most burials at the cemetery up through the 1920s were of people from the Deadwood Creek area. It may have been Deadwood Creek residents who chose the cemetery's location — on flat land near their claims, but in an area unsuitable for mining.

By 1920 the population along Deadwood Creek and its tributaries, as well as along other creeks in the district, had shrunk. This was partly due to consolidation of small claims into larger tracts on which operators could utilize more-efficient large-scale mining techniques and employ fewer workers. The decline was also because of the siphoning of young men into the military during World War I. Many of those leaving Alaska during the war never returned.

Conversely, Central's population grew. Central Roadhouse was rebuilt and enlarged after a 1925 fire, a store and post office were added, and the number of cabins at Central gradually increased.

The burials in the cemetery reflect the economy and demographics of the area. There are few burials of women and children, indicative of their rarity along the creeks. In Ruth Olson's interview she mentioned that her mother was the only adult woman living along Deadwood Creek in the 1910s and early 1920s.

At least a third of those buried in the cemetery were bachelor miners like Jens Langlow (1881-1969), who arrived in the Klondike in 1899 and migrated to Alaska in 1905. For a time he mined on Deadwood Creek with his partner, Nick Knutsen (1876-1949, also buried in the cemetery). Nick was 6-feet-7-inches tall, while Nels was much shorter. According to Connie Jeglum's 2005 publication about the cemetery, the two were known as "the long and short of it."

Several of those interred, like Earl Stout (1891-1983), were employees of the Alaska Road Commission. Stout came to Alaska in the 1920s to work on the railroad bridge across the Tanana River. He also mined in the Yukon River-Charley River region for many years before being employed by the Alaska Road Commission.

There are also several burials related to Central Roadhouse, including those of Alfred "Riley" Erickson (1869-1948) and Adolf "Diamond" Urban (1877-1950). Riley was the roadhouse proprietor, and Diamond was a retired circus clown and the roadhouse gardener.

The cemetery is still in use, the last burial being in 2014. Pioneers of Alaska Igloo No. 4, based in Fairbanks, has replaced six of the cemetery's grave markers. The cemetery is maintained by the Circle District Historical Society, and is open to visitors.

Sources:

- A *Brief History of the People Buried in the Central Cemetery near Central, Alaska*. Connie Jeglum. Fairbanks Genealogical Society. 2005
- Conversation with Leila Coskey, member of Circle District Historical Society
- Correspondence with Erika Miller, member of Fairbanks Women's Igloo No. 8, Pioneers of Alaska
- Deadwood Cemetery Plot Map, Erika Miller, unpublished
- "Ruth and Roy Olson are interviewed by Sylvia Bouillion in Fairbanks, Alaska on January 31 and February 6, 1997." UAF Oral History Collection
- *The Gold Placers of the Fortymile, Birch Creek and Fairbanks Regions, Alaska*. L.M. Prindle. U.S.G.S. 1905

Storage shed and bunkhouse at Deadwood Creek in 2015

Deadwood Creek mining camp near Central survives as family retreat

Deadwood Creek is a 20-mile-long northeasterly flowing stream in the Circle Mining District. It tumbles down out of the mountains before meandering across flats and emptying into Crooked Creek a few miles east of Central.

Reputed to be the "most mined-out" creek in the region, Deadwood has been pretty much continuously mined since the early 1890s. It and its tributaries, along with the Mastodon Creek area to the west, were the two primary gold-producing areas in the Circle Mining District.

Gold was discovered on nearby Birch Creek in 1892 and by November 1893 the entire length of Deadwood Creek had been staked.

When Josiah Spurr toured the area for the U.S. Geological Survey (U.S.G.S.) in 1896, local miners referred to the creek as "Hog'em Gulch," since, as Spurr wrote, "Its discoverer tried to hog all the claims for himself, taking up some for his wife, his wife's brother, his brother, and the niece of his wife's particular friend; even, it is said, inventing fictitious personages that he might stake out claims for them."

At an organizing meeting of miners, the question of naming the creek arose. One miner suggested the "Hog'em" moniker, but cooler heads prevailed and the more dignified "Deadwood Creek" was chosen. However, locals called it Hog'em Gulch for years afterward.

The gold-producing placers of the Circle Mining District are relatively shallow. During the district's early years, operations were typified by individuals or small groups of miners.

These miners used simple methods such as drifting (underground mining of frozen gold-bearing gravels sitting on top of bedrock), open-cut mining (excavating from the surface to reach gold-bearing gravels), and small-scale hydraulicking (washing out gold-bearing gravels using high-pressure jets of water).

According to the U.S.G.S. report, *Gold Placers of the Circle Mining District*, there were 106 claims along Deadwood Creek in 1907, but over the years claims were consolidated as more efficient large-scale mining techniques were introduced.

After 1909, large hydraulic operations were the norm until they in turn were replaced by mechanized operations starting in the mid-1930s. By 1936, only six placer gold-mining operations worked the creek.

Those operations were along the upper portions of the creek, but in the latter 1930s a small dredge churned the gravels along the lower creek. Miners Andrew Olson, Tony Lindstrom and Alex Palmgren formed the Deadwood Mining Company and built a small dredge that operated along Deadwood Creek during 1937 and 1938. The trio moved the dredge to Nome Creek (on the other side of Eagle and 12-Mile Summits) in 1939.

Wrede Brothers Mining Company, sometimes called Deadwood Creek Mining, was one of the few placer operations along the upper creek during the mid 1900s. The four Wrede brothers — Bill, Fritz, Everett and Ray — ventured north to Alaska in the 1930s and settled into mining in the Circle District.

Bill and Ray eventually moved to Fairbanks and operated a dry-cleaning business called College Cleaners. Fritz and Everett stayed in mining and ran a small drag-line operation along Deadwood Creek, just upstream from the confluence of Deadwood and Switch Creek.

They built a small mining camp just above the creek on the downhill side of Deadwood Creek Road. There are six buildings still standing at the camp, all of them wood-frame structures sheathed with tar paper.

A large cook shack and two smaller buildings sit to one side of the road leading down into the camp, with two small bunkhouses and an even smaller storage shed/workshop on the opposite side of the road.

My drawing shows the storage shed and one of the bunkhouses. The camp, typical of small mining operations, is still owned and used by the Wrede family.

Sources:

- Bill O'Leary interview with Mary and Frank Warren at Central 1984. University of Alaska Oral History Collection. (Bill was a long-time Central area resident.)
- Conversations with Pat Babcock and Jeanette Wrede (Ray Wrede's daughters)
- *Gold Placers of the Circle District, Alaska—Past, Present, and Future.* Warren Yeend. U.S. Geological Survey. 1991
- *Mining in the Circle District.* J. B. Mertie, Jr.. In *Mineral Resources of Alaska.* U.S. Geological Service. 1929
- *Yukon Frontiers—Historic Resource Study of the Proposed Yukon-Charley National River.* Melody Webb Grauman. National Park Service. 1977
- *Through the Yukon Gold Diggings.* Josiah Edward Spurr. Eastern Publishing. 1900

The WAMCATS wireless station in Circle as it looks today. It was built in 1908.

How wireless telegraphy helped modernize Circle

The Washington-Alaska Military Cable and Telegraph System (WAMCATS) was an approximately 1,550-mile-long Alaska communications system built between 1900 and 1904. It linked a string of U.S. Army posts: Fort Davis in Nome, Fort St. Michael in St. Michael, Fort Gibbon in Tanana, Fort Egbert in Eagle and Fort Liscum in Valdez.

According to Morgan Blanchard's 2010 doctoral dissertation on WAMCATS, original plans called for running telegraph lines from Norton Sound across the Nulato Hills and up the Yukon River to Eagle, from where a line ran south to Valdez.

Lines reached Rampart by January 1902, but crews struggled fruitlessly to find a route across the Yukon Flats.

An alternate route along Beaver Creek proved equally unfeasible.

Planners decided to run telegraph lines up the Tanana River instead. Crews started work on the new route in February 1902, and a link-up between the line from Nome and the Eagle-Valdez line was accomplished in June 1903.

Telegraph lines never reached Circle, but the community was not forgotten. Wireless telegraphy (radio) began supplementing and then replacing land-lines within a few years of the completion of the WAMCATS. Wireless stations were built throughout Alaska, and in 1908 a station (with a 200-foot tall antenna) was constructed in Circle.

The Circle station was of wood-frame construction, consisting of a 24' by 24' two-story gambrel-roofed section housing offices and living quarters, and a 17' by 24' single-story gable-roofed section where the generator and other equipment were located. Most of the building had shiplap siding, but the gambrel-end of the second story was sheathed with cedar shingles. The building originally had a covered front porch, but only its decking remains.

After Circle's wireless station was completed, lines were run south to creeks in the Circle Mining District. The lines reached as far as Miller House at Mammoth Creek, 45 miles southwest of Circle, and went up many of the creeks.

The telegraph lines were eventually converted to telephone service consisting of one multi-party line. Ruth Olson, a long-time resident of the Central area, related in a 1997 interview that every evening the wireless operator in Circle, as well as everyone with telephone access along the system would get on the phone. The operator called the roll, and someone at each phone location answered. If no one responded, then people knew something was amiss. After roll call, the operator read the daily news from the rest of the territory and the outside world to those listening.

The Army, which was responsible for the system, eventually abandoned most of the land-lines or transferred them to private telephone companies, including the lines from Circle to Miller House. Nels Rasmussen, a Circle-based freighter, became the first private owner of the Circle telephone system.

Because of economic difficulties during the Great Depression, between 1933 and 1935 many of the smaller, non-self-supporting wireless stations in Alaska were shut down. Circle's station was one of those closed.

The Bureau of Indian Affairs, which operated Circle's school, appropriated the building. The generator room became a classroom. Patricia Oakes wrote in an article in the 1983 book, *Education in Alaska's Past*, that with its 11-foot ceilings, about 40 cords of wood per year were needed to heat the drafty, uninsulated building. Even after converting to oil heat it remained impossible to keep the building warm. The state of Alaska took over the school in 1959. A new school was constructed in 1965 and the old building abandoned.

The wireless station still survives, located between Willow and Alder streets a few hundred yards from the Yukon River. Obscured by trees, it sits decaying, with only the moss-covered concrete piers for the long-gone antenna keeping it company.

Sources:

- Conversation with Earla Hutchinson, co-owner of H.C. Company Store in Circle
- "Ruth and Roy Olson interview by Sylvia Bouillion on 1-31 & 2-6-1997." University of Alaska Fairbanks Oral History Collection
- "Teaching Conditions at Circle City: 1896-1966." Patricia Oakes. Alaska Historical Society. In *Education in Alaska's Past*. 1983
- "Wires, Wireless and Wilderness: a Sociotechnical Interpretation of Three Military Communication Stations on the Washington-Alaska Military Cable and Telegraph System (WAMCATS)." Morgan R. Blanchard. University of Nevada, Reno. Doctoral dissertation. 2010

North Pole - Grange Road

North Pole Grange building, on the bank of Badger Slough

North Pole Grange links area with its homesteading history

On March 30, 1867, the Alaska Purchase treaty was signed, ceding Russia's interests in Alaska to the United States. Coincidentally, the same year, the National Order of the Patrons of Husbandry, known commonly as the Grange, was formed in the United States.

On December 4, 1867, seven men, including William Saunders of the U.S. Department of Agriculture, met in Washington D.C. to organize the group. The Grange is an advocacy and service organization that promotes the well-being of families, communities, and agriculture. Since its inception it has been an important voice in lobbying at the local, state, and national level for laws benefiting rural America. The birth of the Cooperative Extension Service, and the extension of free mail delivery to rural areas both came about through Grange efforts.

The Grange was also an early advocate of women's rights. Women in the U.S. were not granted the right to vote in national elections until 1920, but from its beginning in 1867, the Grange has given women the same membership and voting rights as men.

The first Grange in Alaska was organized at Palmer in 1935. That was the year when farmers from Minnesota, Wisconsin and Michigan arrived as participants in the Matanuska Colony, a New Deal agricultural re-settlement project.

Palmer's Northland Pioneer Grange #1 remained Alaska's only local chapter until Don and Alice McKee began homesteading along Chena Hot Spring Road in 1957. The McKees helped organize the Two Rivers Grange #3 in 1960, and the Eielson Area Grange (now North Pole Grange #6) in 1961.

For the first few years of the North pole chapter's life, the Grange met in the North Pole Veterans of Foreign Wars (VFW) building. The chapter was finally able to obtain a 55-year lease on four acres of State land on the bank of Badger Slough, south of Eighth Avenue in North Pole, and along what would become Grange Road.

The lease took effect in May of 1964, and members of the local Grange chapter began work on the Grange hall that fall. The building, which is shown in the drawing, has a daylight basement built of concrete blocks, with a one-story gable-roofed structure with milled-log walls above.

All the work on the building was accomplished with volunteer labor as funds for materials became available. Consequently, building the hall was a multi-year project.

Jeannette Therriault, along with her husband, Hector, were early members of the North Pole Grange. She told me that in 1966, the Grange held meetings in the basement while the first floor was being finished.

Santa's Swingers, a square-dance group to which she belonged, was organized in 1966, and also met in the Grange hall basement.

In 1967, it was members of the Santa's Swingers group who laid down the hardwood floor on the Grange hall's first floor. In keeping with the frugal nature of the building project, the flooring was donated—salvaged from another building that was being demolished.

In the 1960s, the North Pole Grange hall was surrounded by homesteads. Therriault said that most of the major roads in the area, such as Brock, Plack and Hurst Roads, were named after the people who originally homesteaded those areas. The farm equipment located adjacent to the Grange hall came from Ben Coben's homestead along Eielson Farm Road.

The Grange hall became a community center for the area. Many area churches, such as St. Nicholas Catholic Church and New Hope Methodist-Presbyterian Church, held services at the Grange hall until they could build their own sanctuaries. The North Pole Grange still allows other groups to use the hall, and of the chapter's most popular activities is its First-Friday art show, which has been going on for over 10 years.

The North Pole Grange's lease with the State expired in 2019. At that point the people who had been running the Grange in North Pole, recognizing the changed nature of the community, reorganized as a non-profit museum and art gallery. With a new lease from the State, the building is now operated as the Grange Art Gallery

Sources:

- Conversation with Jeanette Therriault, early member of North Pole Grange
- Conversations with John Porrier, former member of North Pole Grange executive committee, now member of North Pole Grange Art Gallery board of directors
- Fairbanks North Star Borough signage at North Pole Grange hall
- "Gallery at North Pole Grange is the picture of success." Amanda Bohman. In *Fairbanks Daily News-Miner*. 5-17-2015
- "History of the Grange in Alaska." Alice McKee. Alaska State Grange website. No date
- "Our Roots." No author. National Grange website. No date

Cliff and Orea Haydon's cabin along Chena Slough in 2014

Haydon cabin evokes memories of homesteading along Chena Slough

The Badger Road area was settled by homesteaders beginning in the early 1900s. However, before homesteaders started clearing land there was just Chena Slough snaking through the birch- and spruce-covered lowlands.

The Alaskan definition of a slough is a river sidechannel, and Chena Slough used to be such a waterway. It branched off from the Tanana River southeast of present-day Fairbanks, upstream from Moose Creek Bluffs, and meandered about 40 miles before rejoining the Tanana where the confluence of the Chena and Tanana Rivers is now.

The Chena River emptied into Chena Slough about 18 miles (as the fish swims) upstream from Fairbanks—a few miles downstream from the current Nordale Road bridge.

In 1901 E. T. Barnette, trying to reach the upper Tanana River aboard the riverboat, Lavelle Young, tried ascending Chena Slough to avoid a rough section of the river called Bates Rapids. Unsuccessful, he and his party were forced to disembark on a bank of the slough. Thus was Fairbanks born.

Low water in Chena Slough routinely plagued Fairbanks-bound steamboats. According to the book, *Steamboats on the Chena*, at one point workers attempted to divert more water from the Tanana River into the slough by opening additional channels at the slough's upper end. Their efforts did little to alleviate low-water levels, and perhaps contributed to the severity of floods that inundated Fairbanks on a regular basis.

Those frequent floods were one of the banes of early Fairbanks, and residents eventually decided that less Tanana River water running through Fairbanks was desirable. In 1945 the flow of water into the slough was curtailed when Moose Creek Dike was constructed, severing Chena Slough into two segments. (Moose Creek Dike is not to be confused with the later Moose Creek Dam and Chena Flood Control Project.)

The slough's upper segment became Piledriver Slough—probably named after Piledriver Roadhouse, located about 30 miles from Fairbanks where the Valdez-Fairbanks Trail crossed the slough. Piledriver Slough, conjoined with Moose Creek, found a new outlet to the Tanana River.

The lower segment of the slough remained Chena Slough. Now it is commonly called Badger Slough. It only has an outlet into the Chena River, and its water source is groundwater seepage from surrounding lowlands.

Chena Slough used to be much wider and deeper. However, without the inflow of Tanana River water, the slough's channel and the Chena River channel have shrunk over the years. Chena Slough shrank more drastically though. Boats could once ply the entire length of the slough, but now only portions are navigable.

According to Bureau of Land Management records, Fairbanks residents began staking homesteads along the slough in the 1920s. One of the earliest homesteads was that of Harry Badger, (Badger Road's namesake) who filed for entry in 1922. His homestead was located about where Nordale Road now crosses the slough. In a 1993 interview with Margaret Van Cleve, Orea Haydon (another Badger Road homesteader and neighbor of Harry) remembers the large fields of strawberries that Harry and his partner, Walter Crick, grew, and the large community dinners the two hosted.

Orea and her husband, Cliff, homesteaded nearby. Cliff filed for entry in 1941, a year before marrying Orea, but World War II intervened and he couldn't make the necessary improvements until after the war. Badger Road ran through their homestead and they grew barley, oats and wheat alongside the road. Orea was also well-known for her extensive flower gardens. Like many homesteaders, the Haydon's worked in Fairbanks to support what Cliff referred to as the "stump farm."

Their home, built during the 1940s, is just off Badger Road on Haydon Court. The original 19' by 25' log structure, with dovetailed corners, faces the slough. An 18' by 21' log addition with saddle-notched corners extends to the rear. All-in-all it is a picturesque reminder of homesteading along Chena Slough.

Sources:

- Bureau of Land Management records
- Cliff and Orea Haydon interview by Margaret Van Cleve on September 1, 1993. University of Alaska Fairbanks Oral History Collection
- "Restoration of Sloughs in the Fairbanks North Star Borough (Tanana River Watershed)". Nancy J. Ihlenfeldt. Alaska Department of Natural Resources. 2006
- *Steamboats on the Chena*. Basil Hedricks & Susan Savage. Epicenter Press. 1988
- "Transforming the Chena Slough through Fairbanks into a River - 1900 to Present." Bob Henszey. U.S. Fish and Wildlife Service. 2015

The single-story portion of North Pole radio station, KJNP, was built in 1967 and looks much the same now as it did then.

KJNP radio and TV celebrates 50th year of broadcasting

KJNP radio and TV celebrated its 50th anniversary in 2017, as its North Pole radio station began transmitting in 1967. However, KJNP's history goes back further.

Don and Genevieve (Gen) Nelson, the station's founders, came to Alaska in 1956 as missionaries based at Stevens Village, a small Athabascan community along the Yukon River northwest of Fairbanks. Don was a Bush pilot, and he and Gen flew regularly to nearby communities to hold services.

In KJNP's booklet, *Miracles in North Pole*, Don tells of flying his Cessna to the Lower 48 one winter to install skis on the plane and of being delayed by bad weather on the return trip. He finally arrived in Fairbanks by mid-December, but a prolonged period of 50 below zero temperatures prevented him from returning to Stevens Village for Christmas.

Instead of making his customary Christmas flights to surrounding villages, he ended up producing a Christmas gospel program transmitted to villages from Fairbanks radio station KFRB. That station, which began broadcasting in 1948, was the town's second radio station.

The program was, of course, heard by others, and with the positive response it received, the station manager asked Don to produce a regular gospel program. Don's radio ministry had begun.

Don was given the opportunity several years later to buy the radio station. When that plan fell through, he and Gen decided to build a radio station instead, and so, KJNP (King Jesus North Pole) was born.

Local homesteader David Ainley donated land for the radio station. With money raised from local residents, the sod-roofed log building to house the radio station was built. Equipment for the radio station, including the transmitter and 420-foot tower, was purchased in the Lower 48 and trucked to Alaska by Don and others using pick-up trucks and trailers. After installing the equipment and erecting the tower behind the station, KJNP 1170 AM, transmitting at 10,000 watts, went on the air on Oct. 11, 1967.

Not long after that the radio station increased its power to 50,000 watts to expand its broadcast area. It took a semi-truck (driven by Don and several friends) to bring the transmitter to Alaska.

Dick Olson, president of Calvary's Northern Lights Mission and the present station manager, told me that waste heat from the 50,000-watt transmitter (with hot-burning vacuum tubes) provided heat for the entire building. (By that time the building had been expanded several times, including a rear addition with second-floor three-bedroom apartment.) He also said that when KJNP switched over to a new solid-state transmitter that cost less to operate, KJNP was forced to install numerous oil-fired heaters to heat the building.

The higher wattage transmitter allowed KJNP's signal to reach locations around the world: Scandinavia and Europe across the North Pole, Russia, Japan, Canada, and as far as Maine in the Lower 48.

On Oct. 11, 1977, KJNP began FM transmissions at FM 100.3. It switched on its TV station on Dec. 7, 1981. The antennas for both the FM and TV transmitters are on Ester Dome.

Regarding the tower for the TV antenna, it was trucked to Alaska in two sections, both strapped to a 50-foot long semi-trailer. The load arrived in Fairbanks during the annual Golden Days celebration, so before unloading the truck, Don and associates hung banners on the trailer and drove their semi-truck with tower in the Golden Days parade.

Don died in 1997 and Gen in 2009, but the work continues. KJNP replaced its AM transmitter tower in 2018 so it could continue its ministry to the top of the world.

Sources:

- Conversation with Dick Olson, president of Calvary's Northern Lights Mission, and general manager of KJNP Radio and TV
- *Historic Fairbanks, An Illustrated History*. Dermot Cole. Fairbanks Chamber of Commerce. 2002
- "KJNP is still in tune after all these years." Nancy Tarnai. In *Fairbanks Daily News-Miner*. 11-27-2000
- *Miracles at North Pole*, Don Nelson. Calvary's Northern Lights Mission. No date

Ladd Field commander's quarters on North Post. Completed in 1941, it is one of the oldest buildings on Fort Wainwright

Ladd Field began life as cold-weather testing facility

Ladd Field, now Fort Wainwright, began as a cold-weather testing facility. Named after Major Arthur Ladd, it was the first U.S. Army airfield in Alaska.

According to the report *The World War II Heritage of Ladd Field*, congressional hearings on U.S. air defenses were held in 1935. At one of these hearings Brig. General Billy Mitchell uttered his now-famous words, "I believe that in the future, whoever holds Alaska will hold the world."

In August 1935 Congress passed the Wilcox Air Base Act, authorizing the War Department to determine locations for future air bases it deemed "essential," with special consideration for, among other things, a cold-weather training facility in Alaska.

A site selection team visited Fairbanks in July and August 1936, and in March 1937 President Franklin Roosevelt withdrew a tract of public land on the banks of the Chena River just east of Fairbanks for the airfield.

Design work began in 1938, and construction funds were approved in early 1939. Crews started work on a railroad spur and road from Fairbanks to the site in August the same year. The rail extension ran from the Alaska Railroad yard north of the Chena River three miles east before crossing the river to the airfield site. The road onto post (later named Gaffney Road in honor of base commander Lt. Col. Dale Gaffney) stretched eastward 3.5 miles along the Chena River's south bank.

The next spring construction of airfield facilities began. Army engineers, unfamiliar with permafrost, naturally made mistakes. For instance, soil beneath the runway was only excavated to a depth of 12 inches, and portions of it heaved and sagged when underlying permafrost melted. This evidently led to quite a few long-time locals wagging their fingers at the Army and saying, "I told you so!"

The affected portions of the runway were quickly redone, this time with 15'-deep excavations backfilled with insulating material. Even with the delays the runway was completed and put into operation in 1940, a year earlier than anticipated.

The buildings on the oldest portion of Ladd Field, also called North Post, were completed next. Located just north of the main runway, North Post was laid out in a formal arrangement borrowed from the Beaux Arts design movement popular in the U.S. from the 1890s to the 1930s. Beaux Arts was a neoclassical style originating in France. While the Old Post buildings' designs are not neoclassical, the site layout, with its open vistas, formal planning, spacing and symmetry is very much in the spirit of Beaux Arts.

The two-story housing units at Ladd Field (including the commanding officer's quarters shown in the drawing) were actually constructed in a simplified American Neocolonial style, while the administrative and service buildings could be considered modern industrial.

Park Service documents state that most of North Post was laid out in a horseshoe pattern around a lawn and parade ground. The horseshoe was bisected by Gaffney Road. North of Gaffney, at the top of the horseshoe, was a semicircular lawn with officers' quarters on the west, north, and east sides. South of Gaffney, on either side of the rectangular parade ground were service buildings. At the horseshoe's base, adjacent to the runway, was Hanger No. One, the operational center of Ladd Field.

The original facilities included nine buildings for administration and housing, six technical buildings, a hospital, and tactical fuel storage. The housing units north of Gaffney road were completed in 1941, but other buildings, such as Hanger No. One, were not completed until 1942.

Hanger No. One's completion two years after Ladd Field officially opened meant aircraft mechanics endured extremely harsh operating conditions those first two winters. Ladd Field's sole mission during its early years was cold-weather testing — not only of aircraft and associated equipment, but also clothing, survival equipment and other military gear.

The entry of the United States into World War II co-opted much of Ladd Field's facilities, but cold-weather testing continued as a primary function until the end of the 1940s.

Sources:

- *Early Transportation Routes, Fort Wainwright, Alaska*. Ronald Burr Neely, Jr. Center for Environmental Management of Military Lands. 2003
- "Ladd Field – National Register of Historic Places nomination form. "Erwin Thompson. National Park Service. 1984
- *The World War II Heritage of Ladd Field*. Cathy Price. Center for Environmental Management of Military Lands. 2004
- *The Forgotten War, Volume Two*. Stan Cohen. Pictorial Histories Publishing Company. 1988.

Hangar No. 1 at Ladd Field as it looked during World War II, circa 1943.

Ladd Field grew rapidly during World War II

Ladd Field began as an Army Air Corps cold weather testing facility. Initial operations began in September 1940 even though the only portion of the field completed by then was the runway.

The three-story Hangar No. 1 (shown in the drawing), completed in 1941, was the post's operational headquarters until the 1950s. The 327' by 271' hangar was the largest structure in Interior Alaska at the time of construction.

A massive aircraft bay ran down the center of the building, and sliding panels could divide the bay in half. Stairwells were located at each corner, and shops and offices lined the bay on its north and south sides. A small third floor office area surmounted by the control tower overlooked the runway.

Even before the hangar was completed, Ladd Field was used for cold weather testing. According to the Center for Environmental Management of Military Lands

(CEMML) document, *World War II Heritage of Ladd Field*, while work progressed on the hanger during the winter of 1940/41, mechanics gained some respite from frigid temperatures by using movable shelters to work on airplanes.

After the United States entered World War II, the Army became increasingly concerned about protecting Alaska from invasion and began diverting resources at Ladd Field from testing to defensive needs. When Japan attacked Attu and Kiska in the Aleutian Islands in June 1942, the Cold Weather Test Detachment (CWTD) at Ladd field was temporarily disbanded.

Personnel and equipment were re-deployed to Nome, where attacks were anticipated, and to the Aleutian military campaign. During the Aleutian campaign three Ladd Field pilots and their crews were lost.

By fall 1942, Gen. "Hap" Arnold, chief of the Army Air Corps and a staunch supporter of the cold weather testing program, had reactivated the CWTD at Ladd Field. The CWTD continued using Ladd Field until after World War II.

Cold weather testing was a vital part of Ladd Field's mission, but another World War II program overshadowed it. In 1942, the field was selected as a transfer point for aircraft and materials headed to the Soviet Union under a Lend-Lease agreement.

The Lend-Lease program was developed to provide war-time materials to Great Britain. The program was gradually extended to other nations, including the Soviet Union.

During the war, 7,926 aircraft were transferred to the Soviet Union over the Alaska-Siberia (ALSIB) route. Planes such as the Bell P-63 Air Cobra (shown in the drawing foreground), and the Douglas A-20 Havoc (shown airborne in the background) flew through Ladd Field.

The newly manufactured planes were ferried by American pilots from Great Falls, Montana along the Northwest Staging Route (a series of airfields stretching across western Canada and Interior Alaska) to Ladd Field.

Ladd Field became a linchpin along the staging route. It was there that aircraft were transferred to Soviet personnel, and prepared for ferrying to the Soviet Union via airfields at Galena and Nome and over the Bering Straits. In addition to other airfield facilities used by the Soviets, Hangar No. 1 was partitioned so the Soviets could use half the hanger, with the CWTD occupying the other half.

Soviet pilots flew the aircraft for the remainder of the odyssey. The program required a sizable contingent of Soviet personnel, including translators, mechanics and technicians. At its peak, about 300 Soviets were stationed at Ladd.

From its modest beginnings as a small cold weather testing facility, Ladd Field grew dramatically during World War II. By the war's end, the post had expanded to several hundred structures. Many of those buildings were temporary and either torn down or re-purposed after the war. Some were moved off-post to become housing for Fairbanks' burgeoning civilian population. A few of those buildings can still be spotted around Fairbanks.

National Park Service documents indicate that there are about 30 structures from the 1940-1945 period still surviving, including two runways, the commander's quarters, officers' quarters, Hangar No. 1 and several other hangars, the North Post chapel, and post radio station. In 1985 these WW II-related elements of the post were designated a National Historic Landmark.

Sources:

- "Ladd Field, National Historic Landmarks Survey." Rolfe G. Buzzell. National Park Service. 1998
- "Ladd Field, National Register of Historic Places Nomination Form." Erwin N. Thompson. National Park Service. 1984
- *The World War II Heritage of Ladd Field: Fairbanks, Alaska*. Cathy Price. Center for Environmental Management of Military Lands. 2004

Fort Wainwright - 9th Avenue

The Arctic Aeromedical Lab building in Fairbanks as it looks today.
It is now houses Bassett Army Community Hospital facilities.

Fairbanks Aeromedical Lab – Cold War-era program that studied living and working in the Arctic

Alaska has been a U.S. possession since 1867. However, not until the 1930s and the military build-up just prior to World War II did the federal government begin realizing the territory's geopolitical significance.

After the war's end, with erstwhile ally the Soviet Union seemingly menacing North America from across the Bering Straits, Alaska assumed greater import. The U.S. government realized how little was known about operating military forces in the far north. Consequently, during the mid-1940s it began a series of initiatives to remedy the nation's lack of readiness to defend Alaska from trans-Arctic aggression.

In addition to increasing the U.S. military's presence in Alaska, the government began projects to gain scientific knowledge about the Arctic and man's ability to operate there. One of those projects was the Arctic Aeromedical Laboratory (AAL). (Other programs begun during that period included the Fairbanks Permafrost Experimental Station, and the Naval Arctic Research Laboratory at Point Barrow.)

Originally organized in 1947 at the School of Aviation Medicine at Randolf Air Force Base in Texas, the AAL quickly relocated to Ladd Field (then Ladd Air Force Base) in Fairbanks. According to a 1961 brochure, *The Arctic Aeromedical Laboratory, its History, Mission, Environment*, the AAL strove "to solve the severe environmental problems of men living and working in the Arctic."

During the lab's early days at Ladd its facilities were based out of Quonset huts. In 1955 a new facility, consisting of a three-story main building that housed labs, library, offices and conference room; a warehouse; and another building that housed a fabrication shop and "small animal colony," was completed next to the base hospital.

The main AAL building, which is eligible for the National Register of Historic Places, is all that remains. This building, shown in the drawing, was constructed in a modified "International Style" of architecture.

Developed in Europe during the 1920s and 30s, the International Style eschewed ornamentation, preferring clean rectilinear lines. Buildings usually featured flat roofs, and cantilevered design elements were popular. Steel, concrete and glass were the dominant building materials. Freed from historic and regional influences and adaptable to varying climates, it had truly international appeal

The style expanded to the U.S. and other regions after World War II, and was popular in the U.S. for government and commercial buildings up to the 1970s.

From its base at Ladd Field the AAL conducted medical and other studies, using both animal and human subjects. Studies were conducted in Fairbanks, sometimes using two "cold" rooms (which are still there) in the main building's basement, and at other sites spread across the state. An undated history of the AAL entitled, *Dispelling the Cold Bugaboo*, contains a map showing 18 research sites beyond the Fairbanks area—some as far away as St. Lawrence Island, Point Barrow and Mt. Wrangell.

The lab, during its peak years, was staffed by 25 to 30 military personnel plus an approximately equal number of civilians. Among other things, the subjects studied included the effects of short-term exposure to cold and hypothermia, the process of acclimatizing to cold environs, frostbite prevention and treatment, the psychological effects of living and working in the Arctic, water purification and sewage disposal in the Arctic, development of survival rations, and testing survival equipment and clothing.

The Air Force transferred Ladd Air Force Base to Army jurisdiction in 1961. Most Air Force functions were moved to Eielson Air Force Base, but the AAL remained in Fairbanks. The Air Force began winding down the lab's operations in the mid-1960s and the AAL was deactivated in 1967.

The building has gone through several occupants since then, but is now again being used for medical purposes. It is now part of Fort Wainwright's Bassett Army Community Hospital complex.

Sources:

- Conversations with Elizabeth Cook, Cultural Resources Manager at Fort Wainwright; and Gary Larsen, Fairbanks Operations Manager for Cold Regions Research and Engineering Laboratory at Fort Wainwright
- *Dispelling the Cold Bugaboo: A History of the Arctic Aeromedical Laboratory, 1947-1967*. Steven Nickollof. Cultural Resources Management at Fort Wainwright, no date (c 2015)
- *The Arctic Aeromedical Laboratory: Its History, Mission, Environment.* Arctic Aeromedical Laboratory. 1961
- "The Lab and the Land: Overcoming the Arctic in Cold War Alaska. Matthew Farish. In *Isis, Journal of the History of Science Society*. Vol 104. No. 1, March 2013
- Tour of the building when it was the Army Corps of Engineers Cold Regions Research and Engineering Laboratory.

Fairbanks - Downtown, Noble Street

Wilbur Brothers sheet metal shop on Noble Street in Fairbanks. The business has been at this site since 1954

Wilbur and sons played a big role in Fairbanks history

Wilbur Brothers Sheet Metal, in one form or another, has been a family-owned Fairbanks business since 1914.

During the winter of 1913-14, Alden Wilbur Sr., who was living in Seattle with his wife and children, sailed to Alaska. Promised a job in Fairbanks, he made the journey alone, planning to send for his family once he became established.

Landing in Valdez, he walked the 360-plus miles along the Valdez-Fairbanks Trail (also called the Richardson Trail) to Fairbanks — a not uncommon feat in the early 1900s. With roadhouses situated every 15-20 miles along the trail, a well-provisioned hiker could, with luck and determination, walk from one roadhouse to the next each day.

After arriving in Fairbanks, Alden Sr. accepted a job in the tin shop at Samson's Hardware. Roy Wilbur, the grandson of Alden Sr., told me that after six months, Alden left Samson's and established A. L. Wilbur Sheet Metal at the corner of Second Avenue and Lacey Street, where the city parking garage is now. He also brought his family north to Fairbanks.

When Alden's son, Alden Jr., joined the business, the business's name morphed to A. L. Wilbur and Son and the shop moved to Third Avenue in the vicinity of the present-day Nerland Building. A second son, Jack also joined the business.

Later, when the Wilbur boys' brother-in-law, Kenneth Bell, joined the team, the business became Wilbur and Bell Company, specializing in plumbing, heating and sheet metal fabrication. The expanded shop moved across the street to Second Avenue. Wilbur and Bell installed all the plumbing in the Northward Building.

In 1954 the business moved one final time, to 1241 Noble St., near Airport Way. According to the book, *Like a Tree to the Soil, a History of Farming in Alaska's Tanana Valley, 1903 to 1940*, that area was first homesteaded by George Kolde in 1908. The neighboring farm to the west was Paul Rickert's. The area remained agricultural until the 1940s and '50s when Fairbanks' burgeoning population forced farms on the city's fringe to either liquidate or move farther out of town. Part of the Kolde homestead was absorbed into Fort Wainwright, and the remainder was developed as Sutherland Subdivision.

The building that became the Wilber brothers' shop was erected in about 1950. It is a 36' by 100' wood-frame gable-roofed structure covered with corrugated metal sheathing — de rigueur for industrial buildings in early Fairbanks. Roy told me there used to be an identical building a few hundred feet to the south that was torn down during the construction of Airport Way.

Growing up, Roy spent considerable time at the family's business. He remembers helping sort through plumbing fixtures in the old wooden bins at the back of the shop. (The bins' final resting place was the Chandler Plumbing and Heating shop on Minnie Street.)

Ken Bell eventually left Wilbur and Bell Company to establish a separate plumbing business, which is when Alden Jr. and Jack changed the business's name to Wilbur Brothers Sheet Metal. The shop is now owned by Alden Jr's son, Roy.

In a 2014 *Daily News-Miner* article, Roy said one of the mainstays of his father's and grandfather's sheet metal business was selling stoves. Now, Roy spends much of his time restoring old stoves.

The historic shop, in addition to the tools of the metalsmith's trade, is filled with history, including a 1917 Ford truck that Doug Colp and Earl Beistline saved from a fire near Manley; the dog sled used by Don Young when he lived in Fort Yukon; and mementos of Irene Sherman, the self-proclaimed "Queen of Fairbanks."

Another of Roy's projects is resurrecting John Miscovich's homemade washing machine from Flat (near Iditarod) for the Pioneers of Alaska. It seems that other people's treasures often find a home in Roy's shop.

Sources:

- Conversation with Roy Wilbur, owner of Wilbur Brothers Sheet Metal
- Fairbanks North Star Borough property records
- *Like a Tree to the Soil, a History of Farming in Alaska's Tanana Valley, 1903 to 1940*. Josephine Papp & Josie Phillips. School of Natural Resources and Agricultural Science, University of Alaska, Fairbanks. 2007
- "Wilbur-Bell provides plumbing." In *Fairbanks Daily News-Miner*, 2-29-1952
- "Wilbur Bros. Sheet Metal turns 100." Robin Wood. In *Fairbanks Daily News-Miner*, 7-20-14

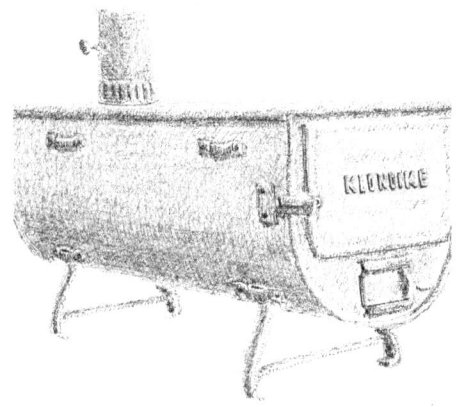

Fairbanks - Downtown, Noble Street

Music Mart in Fairbanks has been a Fairbanks institution for over 50 years. The oldest portion of the building was constructed in 1908

Music Mart: 60 years in the same Fairbanks location

Karl Reinhold Carlson was born in 1922 in British Columbia. His family moved to the United States in the 1930s, and Karl first came to Alaska in 1940 when his family moved to Kodiak, where his father helped construct military facilities during the pre-World War II build-up.

Karl served in the U.S. Navy during the war but returned to Alaska afterward to study mining at the University of Alaska (his father, Carl J. Carlson, was a carpenter, but also mined for gold along Sourdough Creek north of Fairbanks. (See related column in my book, Interior Sketches II).

During high school Karl had become an accomplished accordionist. He even started his own band, the ABCs, with his brothers Arthur and Bert.

His passion for music followed him throughout his life. After World War II, while playing in a band at a USO dance in Fairbanks, he met his future wife, Betty. In the 1950s he put together a band called the Frigid-Aires, which, with a changing membership, entertained Fairbanks audiences for decades

Although Karl studied mining, his heart was in music, and he opened Music Mart in the late 1940s. According to his oldest daughter, Janine Thibedeau, the business bounced around several locations during its first few years.

In 1947, Carl and Betty rented a house owned by Hjalmar and LaDessa Nordale at the corner of Fifth Avenue and Noble Street. Two years later Karl moved his business, which was still quite small, into the front room of the house, and Music Mart has been there ever since.

The house, shown in the drawing, has been added on to over the years, but the original 1 1/2-story wood-frame structure, 30' wide by 52' long, was built in about 1908 by Anton (Tony) Nordale, perhaps best-known for building the Nordale Hotel in downtown Fairbanks. Hjalmar was Tony's son.

Hjalmar died in 1952 and the next year LaDessa sold the house to Karl and Betty.

Karl and Betty raised four children in the Noble Street house. An undated house plan in Fairbanks North Star Borough property records shows the store in the front rooms of the house. The back room, which is now the sheet-music room, is shown as a kitchen/dining room, and the family had bedrooms upstairs.

Betty helped with the business during its early years at the Noble Street location but eventually took employment away from Music Mart to help support the family and her husband's passion. For a time, Betty worked as a medical transcriptionist at Ladd Air Field, and then became a teacher.

The Carlsons lived at the corner of Noble and Fifth until 1967. It was then that Karl, always a wheeler-dealer, traded an organ for a small house that needed to be moved.

Another of Karl's daughters, Barbara Johnson, told me that with Karl having grown up in a family of builders, moving the structure wasn't an obstacle. The Carlsons bought a lot on Front Street in Graehl (across the road from what is now Graehl Park) and Karl trucked the house across the Chena River and set up the family's new home.

The store expanded into the rest of the Fifth Avenue building (which Karl later enlarged), with the second floor eventually housing music classrooms and an instrument repair workshop. Aurora Keyboards, the piano and organ branch of the business (no longer active) moved across Noble Street, finally settling into the old Salvation Army building (now Thai House Restaurant) at 412 Fifth Avenue.

Karl's youngest daughter, Anita Tomsha, who trained as a music instrument repair craftsperson, took over Music Mart in 1985 and has operated it for the past 34 years. The store's inventory has changed to reflect the times, but, with its distinctive signs and loyal customer base, Music Mart it is still a valued part of the Fairbanks community.

Sources:

- Conversations with Barbara Johnson, Janine Thibedeau and Anita Tomsha, who are the daughters of Karl and Betty Carlson
- Fairbanks North Star Borough property records
- Karl Carlson obituary. In *Fairbanks Daily News-Miner*. 6-13-2008
- "Music Mart keeps music, instruments playing." Sam Friedman. In *Fairbanks Daily News-Miner*. 12-20-2015

Fairbanks - Downtown, 3rd Avenue

The Northward Building in 2014

The Northward Building still stands out in downtown Fairbanks

In 1950 Fairbanks, Alaska was still a modest little town of small frame-houses and log cabins. The city's business district, fronting on the Chena River, pretty much fit in a three block by four block area, and the tallest building was the four-story Lathrop Building on Second Avenue, built by Austin "Cap" Lathrop in 1939. (It was also the second building in Fairbanks to have an elevator—the first being the Federal Building on Cushman Street.)

1950 was also the year that one of the largest construction projects in the city up to that time was started. The eight-story Northward Building is credited with being the first apartment house in Fairbanks. It was designed in part to alleviate the city's acute housing shortage, caused by the influx of workers involved in military construction, and of military personnel and their families moving into the area.

Just a few years later the 11-story Hill Building, now the Polaris Building, opened two blocks away. It too, was an apartment building constructed to ease the city's housing crisis.

The Northward Building which is 97.5 feet high, is a roughly H-shaped structure that takes up the entire block between Lacey and Noble Streets, and Third and Fourth Avenue.

In 1950 that location was at the very edge of downtown, and several smaller buildings, including boarding houses, were torn down to make room for the new "high rise."

As constructed, the building had a steel frame with reinforced concrete floors, and was clad with metal siding. When opened in 1952 it included a basement with parking, laundry and storage areas; a first floor with retail shops (including grocery store) and a bank; and seven floors of apartments. It was also the third building in Fairbanks with an elevator.

A 1953 ad in the Fairbanks Daily News-Miner noted that the rent for an apartment was $135 a month, including all utilities. That may have been a hefty sum in the 50s, but the Northward Building, which was essentially a self-contained community, was worth it to many.

Edna Ferber, who patterned the central building in her 1958 book, *Ice Palace*, after the Northward Building, wrote (perhaps exaggerating just a tad bit) that "It was Alaska's first apartment house. People fought to live in it. Townsmen, dwelling in their frame houses and wrestling with the regional problems of heating, lighting, plumbing, water, were madly envious of Ice Palace tenants. There never was a vacancy unless a tenant accommodatingly died, rashly built a new house, or left permanently for Outside."

Ferber's novel, written on the cusp of Alaska statehood, immortalized the Northward as her Ice Palace. Fairbanks became the Interior Alaska city of Baranof, and almost everything she wrote about the city and its people became larger-than-life.

The Ice Palace grew from the Northward Building's eight-stories to fourteen-stories, its utilitarian steel siding replaced by glass blocks that at times, "when the refraction was just right…took on an unearthly blue like the aquamarine tint of the vast Morganstern glacier that lay, a giant jewel, just outside Baranof."

According to the 1978 book, *Ferber, a Biography*, the author made five trips to Alaska conducting research. She became very familiar with the territory and its inhabitants. In addition to "borrowing" settings, she also borrowed real-life people, again—building them into larger-than-life characters for her book. Eva McGown became the novel's Bridie Ballantyne—her social ministry transferred from the Nordale Hotel to the Ice Palace, and Cap Lathrop morphed into the powerful Czar Kennedy.

The city's downtown has grown considerably beyond the Northward Building in the past 60+ years, but the building has changed little. The exterior still looks the same, but the interior was renovated in 2001. Almost all the first-floor shops are gone, replaced by offices for various States agencies, but the upper floors are still devoted to apartments and utilities are still included in the rent.

Sources:

- *Ice Palace*. Edna Ferber. Buccaneer Books. 1958
- *Buildings of Alaska*. Alison K. Hoagland. Oxford University Press. 1993
- *Ferber, a Biography of Edna Ferber and Her Circle*. Julie Goldsmith Gilbert. Doubleday and Company. 1978
- *Fairbanks, a Pictorial History*. Claus-M. Naske & Ludwig J. Rowinski. Donning Company. 1981

Gould cabin on Dunkel Street next to Morris Thompson Cultural and Visitor Center

Dunkel Street cabin is one of the oldest buildings in downtown Fairbanks

The small log cabin shown in the drawing is located at 105 Dunkel Street, just to the west of the Morris Thompson Cultural and Visitors Center in downtown Fairbanks. It is a unique part of the downtown Fairbanks cultural landscape, being one of the oldest structures in the core area that is still in its original location.

When the cabin (now known as the Gould cabin) was constructed about 1910, Dunkel Street was on the edge of Fairbanks, just upstream from the riverfront business district. Photographs of early Fairbanks show a sawmill (gone by 1910) about where the visitors center is now, and at the river's edge end of Wendell Street, just east of Dunkel Street, there used to be the ferry to the small settlement of Graehl across the river, and to the mines in the hills beyond.

The Gould cabin was one of numerous other small homes in the area, and it sat at the corner of Dunkel and West Clay streets. The Dunkel Street district was similar to other residential districts around the town's edges, populated by what Josephine Papp and Josie Phillips, in their book on the history of Tanana Valley agriculture, call "town agriculturists."

They wrote that most homeowners in Fairbanks, "raised gardens and berries, some had greenhouses, and nearly everyone planted flowers around their homes. Several dedicated residents experimented with flowers, shrubs and trees to the extent that much of the beauty found in summertime Fairbanks today is a result of their efforts."

According to the Historic American Building Survey, the first known residents of the cabin were Walter and Mary Ellen Gould who purchased the cabin in 1914.

Mrs. Gould was an avid gardener, raising vegetables to feed the family, as well as flowers — particularly fuchsias. The grounds around the cabin are still planted every year with heirloom varieties of flowers and vegetables that would have been grown there during the 1910s.

The cabin is now part of the Morris Thompson Cultural and Visitors Center, which was constructed in 2008.

The cabin as it now stands is 16'6" wide by 20'6" long, and it is constructed of round spruce logs with saddle-notched corners. It has a low metal-covered gable roof which extends 5'6" out over the front porch.

The interior is divided into two rooms. The Goulds sheathed the wall-logs' interior side with flat-sawn lumber and then decorated with Victorian patterned wall paper. The current configuration depicts the front room as a combination living room/bedroom and the second room a combination dining room/kitchen.

This arrangement may represent the earliest version of the cabin. However Fairbanks North Star Borough property records show that for much of the cabin's life it sported a 16' by 13' wood-frame addition tacked on at the rear, housing a kitchen and small bathroom.

The early cabin sat on a wood sill foundation, but at some point a basement with wood-crib walls was dug. When the cabin was sold to the city of Fairbanks in 2006 for the visitors center project, it was heated by a furnace in the basement.

After the cabin became part of the visitors center project, the kitchen addition was torn down and the basement was filled in. (If you look closely at the exterior back wall of the cabin now, you can see where the logs were shaved flat for the kitchen addition.)

The cabin was then rehabilitated to a version akin to it's original state, and the cabin was decorated with period-authentic furnishings. Staff from the University of Alaska Museum of the North and members of the public and the Tanana-Yukon Historical Society assisted with the rehabilitation and decorating, with the restoration funded in part by the Fairbanks Rotary Club.

The Gould cabin is now one of the most photographed historic structures in Fairbanks. It was added to the National Register of Historic Places in 2020.

Sources:

- "105 Dunkel Street Cabin." Steven M. Peterson et al. Historic American Building Survey. 2007
- Conversation with Sara Harriger, Executive Director of the Morris Thompson Cultural and Visitors Center
- Fairbanks North Star Borough property records
- Signage at the Gould Cabin, and Morris Thompson Cultural and Visitors Centers information
- *Like a Tree to the Soil, a History of Farming in Alaska's Tanana Valley, 1903 to 1940.* Josephine E. Papp & Josie A. Phillips. School of Natural Resources & Agricultural Sciences, University of Alaska. 2007

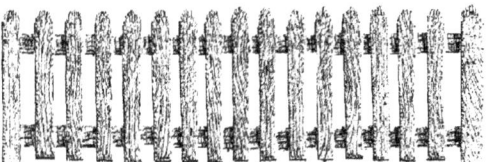

Traditional Athabascan birch-bark canoe on display at the Morris-Thompson Cultural & Visitors Center in Fairbanks.

Modern birch-bark canoe evokes traditional Athabascan culture

The boreal forest (also referred to as taiga) stretches across northern North America, covering much of Alaska and Canada. Paper Birch is one of its signature species, and the region's inhabitants have become adept at using birch bark to construct a variety of implements. Their skills reach a zenith in building canoes.

Both Natives and non-natives constructed birch-bark canoes during the 1800s. The most well-known type of canoe was perhaps the "eastern style," adapted by French-Canadian voyageurs for the fur trade. Similar to modern canoes, they were relatively wide, with slightly rounded bottoms and sides, and curved bow and stern.

Athabascan Indians of the McKenzie and Yukon River drainages by contrast built "kayak-style" canoes with narrow flat bottoms, low flaring sides and angled bow and stern. This type of canoe was well-suited to the region's swift rivers and also required less birch-bark covering—an advantage in Northwestern North America with its typically smaller trees.

These craft had spruce wood frames covered with strips of birch-bark. Split spruce-root lashing held the frame together, and spruce roots were also used to stitch together the bark covering. Seams were sealed with spruce pitch mixed with animal fat.

According to Robert McKennan's ethnographic study, *The Upper Tanana Indians*, most men owned a "hunting" canoe, which was typically 12-16' long, about 24" wide, and very shallow. Canoes across the region usually had birch-bark "decking" across the forward end, however, canoes along the Upper Tanana also featured aft decking.

These canoes weighed about 35 pounds and were easily portaged. They were usually propelled with single-bladed paddles or by poling. Poling wasn't done while standing though. Photos from the early 1900s show seated canoeists working their craft upstream utilizing a pair of long slender staffs—one gripped in each hand.

Athabascans also constructed larger canoes (up to 25' long) for transporting families and cargo. These cargo canoes were similar to hunting canoes, but often lacked top decking.

U.S. Army Captain Charles Raymond, who reconnoitered the lower Yukon River in 1869, also ascended the Anvik River using Native canoes. He wrote that the kayak-style canoes were "admirably adapted to river travel. They are light and draw very little water, and though easily injured they are quickly repaired. In the bow of each canoe a little pitch and birch bark are always kept [for repairs].... The natives make these repairs very rapidly and skillfully, so that an accident ordinarily causes a delay of a few minutes only."

While they were well-matched to their task, Athabascan canoes were finely balanced and took skill to use. Another Army representative, Lieutenant Joseph Castner, wrote in 1896 that he "rode 400 miles in one, but did not feel very secure in any position. It seemed like taking a voyage in a peanut shell."

In the early 1900s canvas began replacing birch bark as a canoe covering but the basic structure remained the same. These canoes were commonly called "ratting boats" since they were used to hunt muskrats. As the ratting boat superseded the birch-bark canoe, so too aluminum canoes eventually replaced ratting boats.

The birch-bark canoe shown in the drawing, which is 18' long, 35" wide, and stands 11.5" high, is a modern re-creation of a traditional kayak-style canoe. It was constructed in 2013 (with locally-harvested materials) in a class sponsored by The Folk School Fairbanks.

The class was taught by Fairbanks resident, Randy Brown, who has constructed numerous birch-bark canoes in both the eastern and kayak styles.

Brown told me that with the myriad variations in canoe building across the region, his did not represent a particular area, but is typical of kayak-style canoes in general. The canoe is now on permanent display in the Morris Thompson Cultural & Visitors Center, at 101 Dunkel Street in Fairbanks.

Sources:

- "A Story of Hardship and Suffering in Alaska." Lieutenant Joseph C. Caster (1886). In *Compilation of Narratives of Explorations in Alaska*. U.S. Government Printing Office. 1900
- *Bark Canoes and Skin Boats of North America*. Edwin Tappan Adney & Howard Irving Chapelle. Smithsonian Institution. 1964
- "Class teaches students the art of traditional birch bark construction." Tim Mowry. In *Fairbanks Daily News-Miner*. 8-15-2013
- Conversation with Randy Brown, instructor for Folk School Fairbanks birch-bark canoe class
- Photos of kayak-style canoes in early 1900s. Clarence L. Andrews Photograph Collection, Alaska State Library Historical Collections
- "Reconnaissance of the Yukon River." Captain Charles P. Raymond, Engineer Corps. In *Compilation of Narratives of Explorations in Alaska*. U.S. Government Printing Office. 1900
- *The Upper Tanana Indians*. Robert McKennan. Yale University. 1959

The Robert and Jesse Bloom house is seen here as it looked in 2007 before it was moved from Third Avenue to Fifth Avenue.

The Blooms, pioneering members of the Jewish community in Fairbanks

After steamers carrying Klondike gold reached the west coast of the United States in 1897, gold fever swept the nation. Thousands rushed north to claim a piece of the bonanza. The nation's small Jewish population was not immune, and according to the Jewish Virtual Library, about 200 Jews made it to the Klondike.

Robert Bloom, a Lithuanian immigrant who first settled in Ireland and then the US, was one of those Jewish sojourners. Hauling trade goods over Chilkoot Pass, he arrived at Dawson in 1898.

Renting a cabin there, Bloom packed his merchandise out to the creeks for miners to buy. When the Klondike rush subsided in 1903, Bloom joined the stampede to Fairbanks. In 1905 he opened a general store in Cleary, and the next year opened a Fairbanks hardware store. The Cleary store disappeared along with most of Cleary in a 1907 fire, but Bloom operated his Fairbanks store until 1941.

Bloom was active in the Jewish community in Fairbanks, which, according to Jesse Bloom's 1963 article, "The Jews of Alaska," was never very large. There were enough Jewish residents to hold services on the Jewish High Holy Days, and a portion of Clay Street Cemetery was set aside for Jewish burials.

Vacationing in Ireland in 1910, Bloom met Jesse Spiro, another Irish Jew. In 1912 the two were married. Back in Fairbanks they raised four daughters and were extremely active in Fairbanks' religious, social, and civic life.

Among his accomplishments, Bloom served on the Board of Regents for the Alaska College of Agriculture and School of Mines, and during World War II was chairman of the Jewish Advisory Board in Alaska. His wife, Jesse, in addition to raising their daughters, helped organize Fairbanks' first kindergarten in 1918, and established Alaska's first Girl Scout troop in 1925.

In 1925, the Blooms bought the house shown in the drawing. The house had been built on Wendell Street around 1917 by a local attorney. The Blooms moved the structure to 523 3rd Avenue, rebuilding it into a luxury home. The wood floors are purported to have been salvaged from a local dance hall.

The 1 1/2-story house is a simplified American Queen Anne-style structure. It includes several distinctive Queen Anne elements such as a steeply-pitched front-facing gable roof, a second story cantilevered out beyond the wall beneath, a porch across the entire front façade, and large windows adorned with decorative leaded-glass. The Queen Anne style was popular from about 1880 through the 1920s.

The house is of wood-frame construction, sheathed with shiplap siding, and has galvanized metal roofing. The first floor is 26' x 34', while the second floor is 26' x 40'. Windows on the side and rear facades are unadorned double-hung sash windows. The front façade's first-floor window is a double window with decorative leaded-glass elements, while its second-floor window is a casement window with transom lights above.

In the first decade of 2000, the building was Aladdin Beauty Salon—sandwiched between the Fairbanks Hotel and Mt. McKinley bank. When Mt. McKinley Bank began work on its new headquarters building on the east end of the block, the Bloom house, along with the Fairbanks Hotel, were slated for destruction.

Fairbanks residents James and Karen Farrell rescued the Bloom house, moving it several blocks to 303 5th Avenue, where it now sits awaiting restoration. Due to the vagaries of life, the Farrells have been unable to restore the building. The old house now awaits news owners to finish restoring it.

Sources:

- "Bloom found refuge, respect in gold rush Alaska." Judy Ferguson. In *Fairbanks Daily News-Miner*. 6-29-2008
- Congregation Or HaTzafon website, < www.orhatzafon.org>
- Conversation with Karen Farrell, co-owner of the Bloom house. 2019
- Fairbanks North Star Borough property records
- "Virtual Jewish World: Alaska—Early History." Jewish Virtual Library website, <www.jewishvirtuallibrary.org>. 1998-2019
- "The Jews of Alaska." Jesse Bloom. In *American Jewish Archives*. November 1963

The Lathrop Building in downtown Fairbanks was once home to the *Daily News-Miner*.

Lathrop Building began as home for city newspaper

Austin "Cap" Lathrop started building an Alaskan media empire with construction of theaters in Cordova, Valdez, Anchorage and Fairbanks during the 1910s and '20s. And in 1924 he produced the silent film, *The Cheechakos* (the first feature film produced entirely in Alaska).

At the end of the 1920s he began branching out into other media outlets. Cap purchased the *Fairbanks Daily News-Miner* newspaper in 1929, and in 1937 began constructing the four-story Lathrop Building (shown in the drawing) to house the newspaper's offices/printing plant.

The downtown Fairbanks building, as with other Lathrop-owned properties such as the Empress and Lacey Street Theaters, was constructed of poured-concrete. Although much simpler in design than his Lacey Street Theater down the block, the Lathrop Building, with its symmetrical design and use of geometric ornamentation, reflects a similar Art Deco influence. It was the second building in Fairbanks to possess an elevator, and there was even a bowling alley in the basement.

According to Elizabeth Tower's book, *Alaska's First Homegrown Millionaire*, the first floor of the Lathrop Building was finished in 1937 and the newspaper immediately moved its offices and publishing plant in.

The second and third floors were completed the next year, and provided 24 deluxe apartments, complete with solid Philippine mahogany doors and built-in china cabinets. Lathrop had originally reserved one of the apartments for himself, but turned it over to one of his newly-married employees who could not find a house or apartment to rent.

The occupants for the fourth floor remained a mystery until June, 1938 when Cap received approval to build a radio station in Fairbanks. By the end of September, 1939 the fourth floor of the Lathrop Building had become the offices and broadcast studio for radio station, KFAR. (The letters stood for "Key for Alaska Riches"). The station's transmitter was located at Mile 5 of the Farm Road (now Farmers Loop). KFAR began broadcasting on October 1, 1939.

Cap found the Fairbanks Daily News-Miner a convenient forum for promoting his political views. However, the radio station took precedence over the newspaper in Cap's interests. Also, the details of operating the newspaper, such as dealing with news-print shortages or upgrading equipment were less to his liking.

A 1980 News-Miner publication by Paul Solka and Art Bremer, *Adventures in Alaska Journalism since 1903*, relates that Lathrop brought Charles Snedden to Alaska in 1949 to conduct an efficiency study for the newspaper. When Snedden recommended spending $100,000.00 on improvements, Cap balked. As an alternative, Snedden suggested that Lathrop sell the newspaper to him. One week before Lathrop's death in a July 26, 1950 industrial accident, the two reached an agreement for Snedden's purchase of the newspaper.

The newspaper's sale was completed after Lathrop's untimely death. With Snedden at the helm of the News-Miner, it continued to operate out of the Lathrop building, and a first-floor expansion was completed in about 1955. The News-Miner remained at that location until a new newspaper plant was built across the river in 1965.

Cap's other business in the Lathrop building, KFAR radio, as well as the building itself, continued to be managed by Lathrop's business associates as part of The Lathrop Company (with the radio station operating under the subsidiary Midnight Sun Broadcasting Company). In 1955 Midnight Sun Broadcasting expanded operations, putting KFAR-TV on the air.

KFAR radio was eventually sold and moved its operations to a different location. However, KATN television, which is the successor to KFAR-TV (but not owned by Midnight Sun Broadcasting), still has its office and broadcast studio on the Lathrop Building's fourth floor.

The Lathrop Building was sold by The Lathrop Company in 1981. It has had several owners since then, but continues to be a landmark in downtown Fairbanks.

Sources:

- *Adventures in Alaska Journalism Since 1903*. Paul Solka & Art Bremer. Commercial Printing. 1980
- *Alaska's First Homegrown Millionaire*. Elizabeth Tower. Publication Consultants. 2006
- Fairbanks North Star Borough property records
- *Historic Fairbanks, an Illustrated History*. Dermot Cole. Historic Publishing Network. 2002

The Tudor Revival-style building that was Claire Fejes' home and art gallery was constructed in the 1930s

Claire Fejes' home and gallery was an artistic haven

When artist and photographer Ernie Wackwitz began construction on his new home and studio at the corner of Cushman Street and 10th Avenue in 1937, the area was on the outskirts of Fairbanks. Paul Rickert's farm was just a few blocks away (where Airport Way is now), and photos from that period show modest frame houses dotting the area.

Wackwitz's building, designed by himself, was much grander than any nearby structures. Buoyed by the city's rising fortunes in the 1930s, the photographer, like many other affluent Fairbanks residents, chose to build a period revival house, inspired by architecture from an earlier time.

His new house, finished in 1939, was Tudor Revival, patterned on English architecture from 1500 to 1559. Wackwitz's home, however, offered a uniquely Alaska adaptation of the building style.

The house's steeply-pitched gable roof, dormer windows, arched entry and front window, tall and prominently displayed chimney, and asymmetrical footprint are decidedly Tudor Revival, but everything is splendidly married to hand-hewn Alaska logs.

The interior was also Tudor Revival, with oak floors, timbered ceilings, leaded glass windows, a massive stone fireplace and open staircase to the second floor. According to a 1999 article by Jan Thacker in the *Great Alaska Journal*, the wide staircase was a popular location for wedding party photos, including those of well-known Fairbanksans, Jo and Dick Scott.

Wackwitz sold the house to Fred Parker in 1942, and the Parker family sold the building to the Boy Scouts of America in 1956.

In 1963, Joe and Claire Fejes bought the house to use as a residence and as a location for their businesses. The Fejeses had been living in a small log cabin and operating businesses from a location on Second Avenue: Joe's hobby shop on the first floor, and Claire, who was an artist, in a small basement art gallery. Yolande, their daughter, told me Joe began stocking art supplies in his hobby shop so that Claire would not be forced to pay retail prices for her paints and other supplies.

After purchasing the Cushman Street and 10th Avenue building, the Fejes remodeled and added on to it, moving the residence to the second floor so Claire could have her gallery on the first floor, with Joe's hobby shop next door. Second floor remodeling also included a studio for Claire, who by that time had achieved success as a painter of rural Alaska Native life.

The Alaska House Art Gallery opened in 1964 with nationally-acclaimed painter and illustrator Rockwell Kent as its first featured artist. Kent lived in Alaska in 1918-19 and wrote and illustrated a memoir of the experience called "Wilderness." It was through his writings that Claire became acquainted with Kent and invited him to Fairbanks. It was also through Claire's efforts that Noel Wien Library acquired its Rockwell Kent artwork.

Claire and Joe retired in the 1970s, selling their gallery name and stock to local businessman and state legislator Charlie Parr. Parr operated the gallery as Alaska House and Xanadu out of the Cushman Street and 10th Avenue location for a time before moving it to Shopper's Forum mall across town.

The Fejes family retained ownership of the Cushman and 10th building, and after the gallery moved out rented it to local businesses. After Claire's death in 1998, her children, Mark and Yolande, decided to reopen the gallery as an archive of their mother's work and to showcase the artwork of a newer generation of Alaska artists. They reacquired the business name and renovated the building, re-opening The Alaska House Art Gallery in 2000.

With the forced closure of the gallery due to the Covid-19 pandemic in 2020, Yolande and her husband, Ron Veliz, decided it was time to retire. Alaska House Art Gallery closed for good in July, 2020, the end of an era for the Fairbanks art scene.

Sources:

- "After more than 50 years, famed Alaska House Art Gallery closing," Gary Black. In *Fairbanks Daily New-Miner*. 7-26-2020
- Conversation with Yolande Fejes, daughter of Claire and Joe Fejes
- *Fairbanks, a City Historic Building Survey*. Janet Mathison. City of Fairbanks. 1978
- Fairbanks North Star Borough property records
- "Keeping the Dream Alive: Alaska House gallery keeps the dream of Claire Fejes alive." Mike Dunham. In *Fairbanks Daily News-Miner*. August 1, 2010
- "Yesteryear elegance: Old Alaska House renamed Joe Fejes Building." Jan Thacker. In *Great Alaska Journal*. 1999, Vol. 1, No. 1 (Aug. 19, 1999)

Fairbanks - Downtown, 1st Avenue

R.C. Woods house on First Avenue in the 1990s

R. C. Wood, one of Fairbanks' neglected early founding fathers

Richard Crowther "Dick" Wood, a pioneer Fairbanks banker and civic leader, was born in Winnemucca, Nevada in 1876. He spent much of his childhood in Tombstone, Arizona where his father built the city's water system and first natural gas plant, and ran a bank.

In 1898, after finishing school, Wood moved to Dawson City as a clerk with the White Pass and Yukon Railroad. (Construction of the railroad wasn't completed until 1901).

He sought richer diggings in 1903 and moved to Fairbanks, securing a job with the Northern Commercial Company as a bookkeeper. During his early years in Fairbanks, Wood also served as City Clerk and was on the board of directors of the *Fairbanks Daily News-Miner*.

In 1906 Wood built a one-story, hipped-roof frame cottage at 927 First Avenue (on the corner of First and Kellum Street). It was a distinctive structure—in a style the book, *Fairbanks, A Historic Building Survey*, calls "Decorated Pioneer House," with a bay window topped by a small gable and large open porch facing First Avenue. Early photos show the house surrounded by an extensive garden.

It wasn't long before Wood followed his father's footsteps into the banking business, becoming a cashier in E.T. Barnette's Fairbanks Banking Company. He left Barnette's employ in 1908, and in 1909 Wood and several other partners purchased a competing bank, the First National Bank of Fairbanks. He was the major shareholder and eventually assumed the bank presidency.

Wood became an aviation enthusiast in 1915 after taking a ½ hour demonstration flight in a Loughead Hydro-aeroplane at San Francisco's Panama Pacific International Exposition. (The pilot, Allan Loughead, become one of the founders of Lockheed Aircraft Company.)

His interest in flying was still high when school teacher and aviator Ben Eielson moved to Fairbanks in 1922. Eielson had temporarily given up aviation, but soon convinced a group of Fairbanks businessmen to purchase a plane for him. The Farthest North Airplane Company, with Wood as president, was formed in 1923 and bought Eielsen's first Alaska plane, a Curtiss-Wright JN-4 "Jenny."

The next year the Fairbanks Airplane Corporation, also with Wood as president, was formed. Noel Wien was the pilot, and Noel's brother, Ralph, was the company mechanic (referenced as a "mechanician" in a newspaper article. (The Wiens established Wien Alaska Airways in 1927.)

Wood sold the bank in 1924, and in 1926 moved to Seattle. He returned to Fairbanks in 1934 as owner of the Fairbanks Agency Company, a brokerage firm.

During this latter period he was on the Board of Regents of the Alaska Agricultural College and School of Mines. He died during a fire in 1944 and is buried at Birch hill Cemetery.

C. W. Snedden and then Gordon Wear owned the First Avenue residence after Wood. They expanded the house by building an attached shed-roofed garage and adding a 1/2 story with gable roof. (The drawing depicts this house.) During that time they continued to maintain the elaborately landscaped yard.

When Gordon Wear died in 1997, Snedden's widow, Helen, re-purchased the property. Inspections showed the structure was too badly deteriorated to renovate so Mrs. Snedden had the building demolished, and a new building roughly following the original floor-plan and in the original style was built.

The new structure is slightly longer than the original and has a full-height second story, but otherwise remains faithful to the original design, including the front porch (now enclosed), bay window and other exterior details.

Helen died in 2012. The current owners still maintain the beautifully landscaped yard and the house remains one of the highlights of the downtown Fairbanks walking tour.

Sources:

- "Bank changes its Ownership and Personnel." In *Fairbanks Weekly Times*. 5-15-1909
- Conversations with Chuck Gray, personal friend of Helen Snedden
- Conversations with Rick Winther, R. C. Wood's grandson
- *Fairbanks, a Historic Building Survey*. Janet Matheson. City of Fairbanks. 1985
- Fairbanks North Star Borough property records
- "Dick Wood is Flying High in San Francisco," In *The Alaska Citizen*. 12-20-1915
- "Our Nome Flyer's are entertained by Organization." In *Fairbanks Daily News-Miner*. 6-23-1925
- R. C. Wood records in Rick Winther's possession

Christian Science church on First Avenue. It was built in 1940 and moved to this site in 1959.

Christian Science one of earliest religious groups active in Fairbanks

In contrast to the more-well-known pioneer Fairbanks churches such as the Episcopal and Presbyterian, another early area church was not one usually associated with missionary zeal and planting new congregations. It was the Church of Christ, Scientist (Christian Science).

The latter half of the 19th century was a time of social upheaval in the United States. New schools of religious thought were spawned as well as revival and reform movements among established religions. Among other religious developments, this period saw the rise of spiritualism and the founding of the Union of American Hebrew Congregations (Reform Judaism) in 1873; the Theosophical Society in 1875; the Church of Christ, Scientist in 1879; and the Church of the Nazarene in 1895.

By the turn of the century, Christian Science was one of the fastest growing churches in the United States. One of its early adherents was Robert Tompkins, who grew up in Michigan and came north to Dawson City during the Klondike Gold Rush. Tompkins worked in mercantile, as well as having some mining interests.

During the 1903 gold rush to the Chena River, Tompkins relocated to Fairbanks. He brought a boatload of merchandise with him from Dawson, which he sold at a tidy profit.

In 1904, he bought two lots near Seventh Avenue and Barnette Street, building a small log cabin on each lot. Tompkins moved into one cabin and stocked the other with Christian Science literature, opening it as a Christian Science Reading Room. (Neighbors were incredulous that he built a church so far out of town.) Informal services were held at the Reading Room starting in 1906.

The congregation soon outgrew its tiny log-cabin home. According to a Sept. 20, 1908, *Fairbanks Daily Times* article, Tompkins led local congregants in building a log addition to the rear of the Reading Room.

The first service in the newly expanded building was held on Sunday, Sept. 13. A newspaper article published the next week stated that Tompkins died 10 days after that service, apparently having worked himself to exhaustion during the expansion.

The first regular meeting of a chartered Christian Science Society in Fairbanks was held on Sept. 18, 1913. I think the number of people who signed as charter members (22) belies the actual size of the congregation — a 1909 photograph shows more than 50 people, dressed in their Sunday best, posed in front of the Reading Room.

The congregation continued to grow. A history of the local church states that in March 1925 it purchased the former Methodist-Episcopal Church building at 603 Third Avenue. (The Methodist Church fell victim to Fairbanks' declining population during the 1910s and closed its doors in 1916.)

The Christian Science church building burned down in 1937, and a new building was constructed in 1940. The congregation was then forced to move their building in 1959, during a downtown urban renewal project.

A lot at 811 First Avenue, beside the Fairbanks Masonic Temple, was purchased. The abandoned two-story building that had originally been the home of E.T. Barnette was already on the lot. That building was torn down, and in the wee hours of Thursday morning, July 23rd, the Christian Science building was move by flat-bed truck the five blocks to its new home.

After it was placed on a new foundation, the building received new siding as well as its distinctive front-façade rockwork. A classroom addition was built at the rear in 1984. The drawing shows this building.

The church is still active. The reading room is on the second floor, and a small sanctuary, with seats from the old Empress Theatre, occupies the middle section of the first floor.

Sources:

- "Christian Science in the New Building." In *Fairbanks Daily Times*. 9-20-1908
- Conversation with Donna DiFolco, member and co-librarian of Fairbanks Church of Christ, Scientist
- "History of Fairbanks Church of Christ, Scientist." Fairbanks First Church of Christ, Scientist. No date
- Fairbanks North Star Borough property records
- "Many Friends Mourn Death of Mr. Tompkins." In *Fairbanks Daily Times*. 9-24-1908
- Photo of Fairbanks Christian Science Church in 1909. Albert Johnson Photograph Collection. University of Alaska – Fairbanks, Archives

Fairbanks - Downtown, 1st Avenue

Some of the Athabascan representatives at the 1915 Tanana Chiefs Conference, from historical photograph

1915 Tanana Chiefs Conference – an early step toward Alaska Native Claims Settlement Act

On July 5 and 6, 1915, one of the precursors to the 1971 meeting of Alaska Native elders at which the pending Alaska Native Claims Settlement Act was discussed, was held in Fairbanks, in the George C. Thomas Memorial Library at the corner of First and Cowles streets.

It was there that 14 Athbascan leaders from lower Tanana River Valley villages met with federal government representatives to discuss impending actions that would affect the Athabascans, and listen to their concerns. The meeting is referred to as the Tanana Chiefs Conference.

According to the 2018 book *The Tanana Chiefs: Native Rights and Western Law,* edited by William Schneider, the meeting came about through the efforts of Alaska's Congressional representative, James Wickersham. Before being elected, Wickersham had lived in Fairbanks, presiding as judge for Alaska's Third Judicial District. He was sympathetic to the needs of the Athabascans, especially with the impending construction of the Alaska Railroad.

Representatives from the Native villages of Chena, Cosjacket, Minto (Old Minto), Nenana/Wood River, Salchaket, Tanana/Fort Gibbon and Tolovana attended the two-day meeting. Another Athabascan, Paul Williams, served as interpreter. The drawing depicts six of the chiefs, plus the interpreter.

Rev. Guy Madara, who was priest at the Salchaket Episcopal mission, also attended. He filled the role, of what Bill Schneider called, a "cultural broker ... attempting to reinforce and explain comments by the Native leaders."

Besides Madara and Wickersham, government agents, H. J. Atwell and Thomas Riggs, were also participants. The first day's agenda focused on land issues.

According to the transcript of the meetings, Atwell, with the government Land Office, told the leaders that the government could help them apply for Native homesteads or establish reservations (the two government-preferred options for dealing with Native land issues). Riggs, responsible for building the Alaska Railroad, told them that after the railroad was completed, the country would be, "... overrun with white people. They will kill off your game, your moose, your caribou and your sheep ... the Indian must protect himself by one of the methods which has been outlined."

After hearing from government officials, the chiefs conferred and most decided that neither homesteads nor reservations were desirable. Homesteads would require Natives to live year-round away from each other, destroying Native communities, and the chiefs believed reservations would not support their subsistence lifestyle.

Chief Alexander of Tolovana told the government representatives that, "... we are people that are always on the go, and I believe that if we was [sic] put in one place we would die off like rabbits."

Chief Joe of Salchaket added, "We are suggesting to you just one thing, that we want to be left alone."

Since further discussions on land issues appeared futile, the next day was devoted to other concerns of the chiefs, including the chiefs' desire for trade schools to teach marketable job skills, better access to wage jobs, better health care, and representation in decision-making that affected them.

At the end of the meetings Wickersham promised to pass the chiefs' concerns on to the Secretary of Interior.

There were no concrete actions that came out of the conference, but it represented one of the first times that Natives had been consulted on issues that affected them. It also showed the chiefs' resolve to speak out on important issues and become involved in representing their people and lobbying for change. From small steps like this, Alaska Natives developed a voice and a unity that eventually led to real changes such as the Alaska Native Land Claims Settlement Act.

Sources:

- "How Athabascan leaders crafted the Tanana Chiefs Conference." Matt Buxton. In *"The Fairbanks Daily News-Miner",* 6-12-2019
- "Proceedings of a Council, Fairbanks, Alaska, July 5, 1915." Wickersham State Historic Site Manuscripts, Alaska State Library Historical Collections.
- *The Tanana Chiefs, Native Rights and Western Law."* William Schneider, Thomas Alton, Will Mayo, Natasha Singh & Kevin Illingworth. University of Alaska Press. 2018

Pan American Airways hanger at Weeks field in the early 1940s

Old Pan American hanger is a piece of Fairbanks' hidden history

The Pan American Airways hangar shown in the drawing is part of Fairbanks' hidden history. It was once used by Pan Am at Weeks Field (located where the Noel Wien Library is now) which was Fairbanks' original airport.

According to Dermot Cole's book, *Fairbanks, a Gold Rush Town that Beat the Odds*, Weeks Field began as a baseball diamond called Exposition Park, and was also used as a race track. Years before it officially became an airport, however, it saw use as a landing strip. In 1913 it was the site for the first airplane flight in Alaska when local merchants brought a husband-and-wife flying team and their airplane to Fairbanks for demonstration flights. The plane arrived in Fairbanks in a crate, and after the flights, it was crated back up for return shipment to the Lower 48.

In 1920, the baseball diamond/race track again was used as a landing field when a flight of four U.S. Army bombers, the Black Wolf Squadron, visited Fairbanks during a 9,300-mile round-trip flight from Mitchell Field, New York, to Nome. It was the site where Ben Eielson made his first flights in his Curtiss-Wright Jenny In 1923.

As the site was used increasingly as a landing field, the city decided serving the needs of aviation should be the site's primary function and established Weeks Field. The

Territory also was realizing the importance of aviation, and in 1925 the Territorial legislature authorized the Alaska Road Commission (ARC) to add airfield construction and maintenance to its list of responsibilities. By 1927, the ARC was maintaining 24 airfields.

Several small regional air carriers were based out of Weeks Field during its earliest years. In 1932, Pan American Airways moved into the Alaska market, buying out Alaska Airways and Pacific International Airways and merging them into a Pan Am subsidiary called Pacific Alaska Airways (PAA). According to a 1991 article in Alaska Business Monthly magazine, the acquisitions provided PAA with facilities in Anchorage, Fairbanks and Nome; and airmail contracts to deliver mail to communities in the Interior, on the Kenai Peninsula and in Western Alaska.

The next year PAA constructed a modern hangar in Fairbanks. As PAA and other carriers expanded and brought larger aircraft into Weeks Field, the airport's runway was lengthened. A gravel runway eventually extended westward from Gillam Way almost as far as the present location of the Fairbanks Curling Club on Second Avenue. In 1941, the name PAA was phased out as the carrier became the Alaska Division of Pan American Airways.

PAA and Pan American used larger aircraft such as the Lockeed Electra for regularly scheduled service between larger communities. Smaller planes such as the Fairchild Pilgrim 100B (NC 7-42N) shown in the drawing were used for flights to smaller airfields in rural Alaska.

These sturdy little planes sometimes are called American Pilgrims since American Airlines purchased most of them. The planes were well known for their short field capabilities, and many of them eventually migrated to Alaska and the Yukon Territory. Only 26 Pilgrim 100As and 100Bs were manufactured, and the sole surviving airworthy Pilgrim is located in Anchorage at the Alaska Aviation Heritage Museum.

By the late 1940s, community expansion in Fairbanks was beginning to envelop Week's Field. That and the need for even longer runways and expanded facilities to serve newer aircraft brought about the development of Fairbanks International Airport.

By 1951, the new airport was operational and Weeks Field closed. Within months of the field closing, the old control tower burned down. The old Pan Am hanger was acquired by a partnership of Fairbanks residents, and in 1959 was re-purposed into what you see today, the Arctic Bowl bowling alley.

Sources:

- "Abandoned and Little Known Airfields in Alaska." Paul Freeman. *Abandoned and Little-known Airfields* website. 2003
- "Alaska's Heritage: Chapter 4-12: Air Transportation." Alaska Humanities Forum website. 2015
- *Fairbanks, a Gold Rush Town that Beat the Odds*. Dermot Cole. University of Alaska Press. 1999
- "New Bowling Emporium is one of Largest in Alaska" In *Fairbanks Daily News-Miner*. 9-28-1959
- Photos and information on Pacific Alaska Airways Pilgrim 100Bs, on Ed Coates Civil Aircraft Photo Collection website.
- "Tales of Pan American World Airways." Kate Ripley. In *Alaska Business Monthly*. July 1991

Fairbanks - Downtown, 2nd Avenue

Fairbanks' First United Methodist Church is the successor to St. James Methodist church, which was established in 1906

Methodist church, forced to close in 1916, is reborn 36 year later

The Christian Church's *New Testament*, through various passages, relates that in spreading the gospel, some may sow, others may nurture, and yet others may reap. So it was with the Methodist Church in Fairbanks, After planting a church, the denomination was forced by declining population to leave the community for several decades before returning to continue the work it had started.

The Rev. John Parsons, a minister in the Methodist Episcopal church, first arrived in Fairbanks, according to his diary, on a Sunday afternoon in August 1905. (The Methodist Episcopal church was the largest Methodist denomination in the United States at that time. The Episcopal in the title refers to the church's governance — having an Episcopal or hierarchical form of government.)

The reverend received a hearty welcome from the community but was cautioned by S. Hall Young, pastor of the Presbyterian Church. Presbyterians and Methodists, while differing on some theological points, are similar in outlook and demeanor. (The old joke is that Presbyterians are just Methodists who can't sing, and Methodists are just Presbyterians who can't spell.) Dr. Young believed that Fairbanks, being a mining camp, would eventually decline, and the town would end up with two struggling churches rather than one strong one.

Parsons was unperturbed and established St. James Methodist Episcopal Church. Fairbanks newspapers from that period report that Methodists built their church at 603 Third Avenue in 1906, just down the street from the city hall and fire station. The church escaped the disastrous 1906 fire that destroyed most of downtown Fairbanks, even serving free meals the day of the fire and the following day.

The back of the church faced Fairbanks' red light district across the alley. Everett Patton, the son of the Methodist church's second pastor, wrote of his first night in Fairbanks, before the family moved into the parsonage, and of his (7-years-old at the time) and his 5-year-old brother's attempt to sleep in the back of the church while his parents attended a welcoming reception in the church sanctuary. Attracted by the sounds of conversation outside, the two boys moved a table against the back wall of the kitchen, put chairs up on the table, and climbed up to look out the high transom windows at the ladies gathered across the alley in their "bathrobes." The next day, their parents, realizing that it was a group of working girls their sons had observed, quickly boarded up the transom windows.

St. James lasted into the mid 1910s, when, as Dr. Young had predicted, Fairbanks population began declining. Church membership plummeted. Rev. Patton was transferred to Seward in 1916, and the remaining Methodists moved to the Presbyterian Church. Shortly after that, St. James Church was leased and eventually sold to the Church of Christ, Scientist.

In 1939, the Methodist Episcopal Church merged with several other Methodist denominations to form The Methodist Church, which would eventually become the United Methodist Church.

In the early 1950s, Methodists ventured back to Interior Alaska. The Methodist Church held its first church service at Carpenter's Hall, 307 Fifth Avenue, in March 1952. They continued meeting there until a new church building was constructed.

Ground was broken at the church's present location, 519 Second Avenue, in June 1953, and the first services in the almost completed sanctuary were held that December. In addition to a full basement, the church had a first floor sanctuary with vaulted ceiling, topped by a steeply-pitched gable roof surmounted by a belfry. Because of its color scheme, parishioners called it their "little brown church," (as in the song, "Little Brown Church in the Vale.")

A Christian education wing (with basement and ground floor) was begun in 1958 and completed in 1966. In 1982 another wing, designed to blend with the existing structure, was added at the rear of the sanctuary. The drawing shows the church as it looks today.

Sources:

- 1906 articles in *Fairbanks Daily Times* newspaper,
- "Diamond Jubilee Festival is Sunday." Virginia Doyle Heiner. In *Fairbanks Daily News-Miner*. 8-7-1982
- Diary of John Parsons. In Fairbanks First United Methodist Church archives. No date
- *S. Hall Young of Alaska: The Mushing Parson*. S. Hall Young. Fleming H. Revell Company. 1927
- Newspaper article by Everett Patton in Fairbanks First United Methodist Church archives, no date, no publisher listed
- "Silver Anniversary Banquet" brochure. No author. In Fairbanks First United Methodist Church archives. 1977

South Fairbanks - Lathrop Street

One of the 1970-era houses at Eskimo Village as it looks today

'Eskimo Village' survives on Lathrop Street

During and right after World War II there was a rapid influx of people into the Fairbanks area as the U.S. military expanded its presence. With the increased demands on the Alaska Railroad during the war and during the "Cold War" era that followed, the railroad also expanded its operations during this period.

To house some of its new workers, in 1946 the railroad began erecting temporary housing on railroad property near the freight yards. That housing consisted of "Jamesway" huts. These prefabricated structures had the same design as Quonset huts. However, instead of metal ribs and galvanized metal sheathing, Jamesway huts were more tent-like, with wooden ribs covered by insulated fabric. By the end of the war there were at least 20 huts on railroad property. The 16' x 32' structures were electrified but not plumbed.

Some of the new railroad workers were coastal Eskimo, primarily Inupiat from Northwestern Alaska, but also a few Yupik from the Kuskokwim Delta area. According to a 1981 University of Alaska master's thesis by Gay Ann White, in the mid-1940s about 110 Eskimo lived in Fairbanks, including 21 complete families.

Six Inupiat families, as well as numerous single Inupiat males moved into the railroad housing, which became known as "Eskimo Village." In 1948, workers were still living in the huts which by then had become dilapidated.

The railroad replaced the structures in 1949 with military-surplus "Dallas huts," 16' x 16' prefabricated buildings constructed of 2x4 framing and plywood, with shallow-pitched hipped roofs. The "new" Eskimo Village was erected near the railroad's engine house. Again, the huts were electrified but not plumbed.

Ten years later, most railroad workers lived off railroad property, but seven Inupiaq families still lived in Eskimo Village. Sanitation was deplorable and the Dallas huts had deteriorated to the point they were not worth repairing. The railroad needed to expand its Fairbanks facilities and decided to close Eskimo Village. In May of 1960 it gave its tenants notice to vacate by June 1, 1961.

It was at that point that the Presbyterian minister in Fairbanks, Brian Cleworth, stepped in to help the families. Presbyterians have a long history of working among the Inupiat (a mission was established at Barrow - now called Utqiagvik - in 1890), and some Eskimo Village residents attended Cleworth's church. Brian told me he was also familiar with Inupiat culture through his work with the church's Board of Missions.

Cleworth spearheaded efforts to obtain housing for the families, working closely with the railroad, the Bureau of Indian Affairs, and the Bureau of Land Management (BLM).

The families desired to stay together. As a result, Eskimo Village was relocated to a small tract of BLM land between 25th and 27th Avenues along Lathrop Street. There is even an "Eskimo Village Road" that shows up on maps. The land was obtained under the 1906 Alaska Native Allotment Act.

The railroad sold the Dallas huts to families for $1 each. It then moved and set up the huts at the Lathrop Street location. As with the railroad location, the huts were electrified but not plumbed. The relocation was completed by October 1961.

Moving to the new location did not end the families' travails though. The 1967 Fairbanks flood severely damaged their homes (they were only elevated off the ground by wooden sills) and all the structures had to be replaced in 1969 and 1970. New 20' x 31' wood-frame houses were constructed on concrete foundations on top of gravel pads.

Because of the poor soil conditions in the area, extending sewer and water lines to the houses was very expensive. It was not until 1974 that they were hooked up to the municipal sewer and water system. Almost 30 years after the Inupiat families moved to Fairbanks, Eskimo Village finally had running water and modern sanitation facilities.

Sources:

- Conversation with Brian Cleworth, Presbyterian minister in Fairbanks during relocation of Eskimo Village
- "'Eskimo Village,' and ethnic enclave in Fairbanks, Alaska." Gay Ann White. University of Alaska, Fairbanks master's thesis. 1981
- Fairbanks North Star Borough property records.

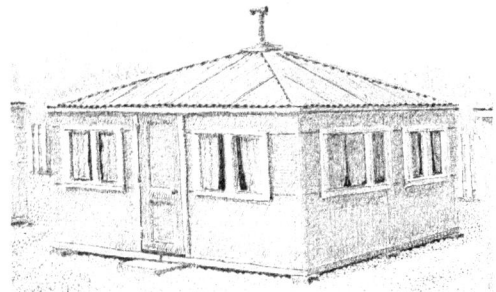

The Alaska Centennial Center for the Arts, at Pioneer Park, was built in 1967 as the Civic Center for the A-67 Exposition

A-67 Exposition survives as Pioneer Park

The 1967 centennial celebration of the United States' purchase of Alaska from Russia was a year-long event in Alaska. An Alaska Purchase Centennial Commission was established in 1963 to coordinate centennial events across Alaska, and 18 communities set up their own committees.

While local events around the state were encouraged, an official state-sanctioned exposition with representation from across Alaska was envisioned. Early in the planning process, Fairbanks threw its hat into the ring as the exposition location, citing, in part, the availability of the 44-acre Pioneer Memorial Park at the corner of Airport Way and Peger Road.

Pioneer Memorial Park had been established in the early 1960s by the Fairbanks men's chapter (Igloo No. 4) of the Pioneers of Alaska. One of the goal of the Pioneers, since the organization's 1907 inception, had been to help preserve Alaska's history. Seeing the accelerated loss of historic buildings and artifacts from the Fairbanks area after World War II, Igloo No. 4 requested public land from the state for a museum and historical park. The 44-acre Airport Way/Peger Road parcel was transferred to the Pioneers through the University of Alaska.

Fairbanks was chosen as the site for the official centennial exposition in the summer of 1964, and the local "A (Alaska) 67" organization was formed. The Fairbanks architectural firm of Gray, Rogers and Cotting designed the exposition site.

Plans proceeded pell-mell, and construction on A-67 facilities began in 1966. With the exceptions noted below, the facilities constructed in 1966 are still there today, including:

• Crooked Creek and Whisky Island Railroad — with one mile of narrow-gauge tracks around the park.

• The riverboat Nenana — retired in 1954. In the early 1960s it was moored along the Chena River near the present-day Aurora Energy powerplant. In 1966 it was maneuvered through a hastily-dug canal to its new resting place. The boat was rehabilitated, and the top deck turned into a restaurant.

• Gold Rush Town and Mining Valley — developed using historic buildings and equipment from the Fairbanks area.

• The Gold Dome — the federal government built this 100-foot-diameter geodesic dome to display exhibits from federal agencies active in Alaska. (The structure now houses the Pioneer Air Museum.)

• The Caribou Corral (where Moose Creek Pavilion is now) — a five-acre enclosure home to a small caribou herd. According to the A-67 publicity packet, plans originally called for moose, reindeer, caribou, musk-oxen and bison to share the enclosure.

• Bonanzaland (where the playground is now) — a midway with concessions.

• Pioneer Hall and The Big Stampede — this concrete-block building, covered with wooden siding and an old-timey false-front, was constructed for Pioneers of Alaska activities, and to house The Big Stampede, a rotating diorama featuring 15 historical paintings by Rusty Heurlin.

• Native village and museum — reconstructions of Native dwellings from around the state, plus a museum housing a temporary collection of Native artifacts from museums around the world.

• Harding Car — the railroad coach used by President Warren G. Harding during his 1923 Alaska visit.

• Civic Center — designed by Philleo Engineering of Fairbanks. The *Alaska 67 Official Guidebook* states that the 140'-diameter building was designed to resemble a Southeast Alaska tribal hall, although some have noted its resemblance to a birthday cake. There are 12 large plaques around the exterior with Alaska Native-inspired images. Designs were provided by noted Native artists such as Joseph Senungetuk and Peter Seeganna. The interior contained exhibit areas, a 388-seat theater and art gallery.

The A-67 exposition was a success, marred only by the August 1967 flood that inundated Fairbanks. But the exposition park survived, morphing into Alaskaland and then Pioneer Park, and is now a vital part of Fairbanks culture.

Sources:

- "A-67" publicity packet, and "Centennial Press" newsletters in Alaska Purchase Centennial Commission collection in University of Alaska Fairbanks Archives.
- *Alaska 67 Official Guidebook.* Alaska 67. 1967
- "Alaskaland Development Plan: 1980s – Decade of Alaskaland." City of Fairbanks. 1979
- Correspondence with Donnie Hayes, Manager of Pioneer Park

Small draglines like this were once common at placer gold-mining operations

P&H dragline at Pioneer Park represents early 1900s industrial innovation

When gold was discovered in Alaska at the end of the 1800s, it was individual miners who initially exploited the resource using picks and shovels and other rudimentary equipment. As easy diggings disappeared, individuals were supplanted by companies with the necessary capital to invest in more-efficient, large-scale gold recovery methods.

These larger-scale operations were aided in the early 1900s by new innovations in earth-moving technology. For instance, incremental improvements to internal combustion engines during the latter 1800s gradually led to smaller, more powerful engines that eventually replaced steam as the motive power in many industrial applications.

At the beginning of the 1900s mechanized mining equipment such as hoists and tractors were powered by steam. However, by the mid-1910s bulky steam engines were being replaced by smaller diesel and gasoline engines.

Coupled with improvements to internal combustion engines was the development of continuous-tracked vehicles, the culmination of decades of tinkering. The first usable crawler-tractors began appearing in about 1907 and quickly found a niche in the mining industry.

Another important innovation was the dragline excavator, commonly just called a dragline. A dragline is an earthmoving apparatus in which a bucket is suspended by cables from a movable boom. The boom, in turn, is mounted to a chassis housing an engine and control cab. Small draglines were commonly mounted on tracks or the back of trucks.

In operation the dragline bucket is maneuvered into position and then lowered to the ground and dragged along the surface, scooping up material. The full bucket is then raised and emptied into a truck bed, train car, or hopper; or dumped at another location. Separate cables are used to position the boom, raise and lower the bucket, and drag the bucket across the ground.

According to a Wikipedia article on dragline excavators, skilled dragline operators could throw or "backcast" a bucket farther than the end of the boom. By pulling the suspended bucket towards the cab and then releasing the drag cable, the bucket would swing like a pendulum. Once the bucket passed the vertical in its forward swing, the hoist cable was released, casting the bucket up to half-again the distance from the cab to the end of the boom.

Draglines were developed in the first few years of the 20th century and by 1910 several U.S. firms were manufacturing them. Those first draglines were powered by steam, but a history of the P&H Mining Equipment Company (started by Alonzo Pawling and Henry Harnischfeger) states that in 1914 the company introduced the first gasoline-engine-powered dragline.

Draglines like the small P&H Model 150 shown in the drawing (now in the Mining Valley at Pioneer Park) were once common at placer mining operations around Alaska. Unfortunately, many of Pioneer Park's records were lost during the 1967 flood, so little is known about the park's dragline.

P&H's Model 150 was a small dragline manufactured between 1937 and 1952. It weighs about 15 tons, has a 30' boom, and a 5/8-cubic-yard bucket. Other manufacturers, including Bucyrus-Erie and Insley, produced similar draglines.

Based on old photos in the Circle District Historical Society photo archives, it appears that draglines were often used in conjunction with bulldozers for loading hoppers on elevated sluice boxes. A 1996 U.S.G.S. report on Fortymile River placer mining states that mines using dragline-bulldozer-hydraulic combinations were active in the 1950s, and that draglines were utilized at least into the 1970s.

In modern small-scale placer mining operations, draglines have mostly been replaced by front-end loaders and backhoes. Small draglines are no longer manufactured, and for the most part, the only operational draglines are giants such as Usibelli Coal Mine's 2,100-ton "Ace-in-the-Hole" dragline at Healy.

Sources:

- "A History of P&H Mining Equipment, Inc." P&H Mining Equipment, Inc. No date
- "Dragline Excavator." Wikipedia. 12-21-2020
- *Gold Placers of the Historical Fortymile River Region, Alaska*. Warren Yeend. U.S. Geological Survey. 1996
- Photos of draglines in operation, in the Louis Smith collection of the Circle District Historical Society photo archive

Fairbanks - Pioneer Park

The Gold Dome, which now houses the Pioneer Air Museum, was built for the 1967 Alaska Centennial Exposition.

Pioneer Park's Gold Dome morphs from white elephant to air museum

Nestled in the heart of Pioneer Park is the Gold Dome, which began as an exhibition venue for the A-67 (Alaska 1967) centennial exposition. It was not the exposition's sole exhibit space, though.

When the exposition opened in spring 1967, a plethora of exhibits awaited visitors. Exhibits showcasing cities and regions of Alaska were housed in the civic center in the Alaska Centennial Center for the Arts.

Another exhibit hall, the U.S. Pavilion, was situated just northwest of the civic center, where the square dance picnic pavilion is now. That was a 100'-diameter, 35'-high silver geodesic dome. Geodesic domes, popularized by Buckminster Fuller, are hemispherical structures with shells of interlocking triangles. The rigid triangular elements distribute structural stress throughout the dome, making it extremely strong and eliminating any need for internal supports. Another example of a geodesic dome built during the same period is the United States pavilion for the 1967 World's Fair.

The U.S. Pavilion at the A-67 Exposition housed exhibits highlighting federal agencies in Alaska. It was evidently a temporary structure that was disassembled after the exposition closed.

Directly northwest of where the U.S. Pavilion used to be is Seward Hall (now called the Gold Dome). It is another geodesic dome. Planned as a permanent structure, the 132'-diameter, 38'-tall building has a metal exoskeleton. The base of the dome is sided with cedar shakes, while the upper roof is covered by gold-colored anodized-aluminum panels.

According to the *Alaska 67 Official Guidebook*, the Gold Dome showcased Alaska's industries and commercial activities. It also hosted other exhibits, including those of Canada and the Port of Seattle.

After the exposition closed, most exhibits disappeared, and the exhibit spaces became available for other uses. Due to a shortfall in construction funds, only the Civic Center's gallery and theater were heated during the exposition. Consequently, the building's exhibit space was unusable during cold weather until heating was retrofitted.

The Gold Dome faced a similar situation. Its only heating source during the exposition was a central fireplace. Oddly, even with the facility's deficiencies, a 1968 *Daily News-Miner* article advertised the facility as available for sporting and theatrical events. It also mentioned that the building gave Fairbanks the capability of hosting conventions.

The facility was indeed used for civic events such as dances, dog shows and Octoberfest celebrations. However, the park's 1979 development plan mentioned that the building did not lend itself to easy use and was viewed by many as a white elephant. A proposal was floated in 1980 to turn the building into an aurorium and exploratorium, but that plan never came to fruition.

Several years later, the Interior and Arctic Aeronautical Foundation (I&AAF) became the building's permanent tenant. The I&AAF had been formed to promote the preservation of Interior Alaska's aviation heritage, and in 1984 the city of Fairbanks, which owned the park, offered the Gold Dome to the I&AAF as a venue for an aviation museum.

The organization began fundraising to convert the Gold Dome into an aviation museum, anticipating that the museum could be open within two years. However, the transfer of the park from the city to the North Star Borough, as well as remediation work on the building, postponed the museum's opening. The Pioneer Air Museum finally opened in 1992.

The museum is one of the top-rated attractions at Pioneer Park. Pete Haggland, the museum's director, told me that the museum desires to improve visitor experiences by enlarging the entrance to accommodate education programs and configuring the entrance to mimic an aircraft hangar, and by adding an aircraft restoration workshop. With those improvements, hopefully the museum will continue to serve visitors for years to come.

Sources:

- *Alaska 67 Official Guidebook*. Alaska 67. 1967
- "Alaskaland Development Plan: 1980s – Decade of Alaskaland." City of Fairbanks. 1979
- Conversation with Pete Haggland, director of Pioneer Air Museum
- *Fairbanks Daily News-Miner* articles, 6-7-1967, 8-8-1967, 6-12-1968, 5-24-1980
- "New Fairbanks museum preserving aviation history, heritage." Jim Magowan. In *General Aviation News & Flyer*. Vol. 44, No. 19 (Sept. 1992)

Fairbanks - Pioneer Park, Gold Rush Town

Tall cache that used to stand at Pioneer Park in Fairbanks

Tall caches were once common in Alaska

In modern Alaska, elevated storage caches (sometimes called fish or bear caches) typically consist of small rustic log cabins built atop four canted legs, above the reach of pilfering animals and attainable only via removable ladders.

They have become ubiquitous symbols of Alaska — some would say hackneyed symbols. The folklorist Susan W. Fair, who referred to these structures as "tall caches," wrote that well-known Alaska artist Byron Birdsall believed depictions of tall caches had become trite, and for most of his career he refused to paint them. When he finally did a cache painting, in a play on words he titled the original watercolor, "The Great Alaska Cliche." (For sales purposes the reproduction of the painting was renamed "The Great Alaska Cache.)

In a 1997 article, "Story, Storage, and Symbol," Fair states that Alaska Natives used elevated storage racks prior to western contact, but that the origin of tall caches — elevated platforms topped by storage sheds — is debatable. They may have been an indigenous development, but Fair hypothesizes that tall caches were probably introduced by Westerners, perhaps on the Kenai Peninsula in the 1870s. They might also have been brought by the Hudson's Bay Company when it established Fort Yukon in 1847.

If tall caches were a Western introduction, they spread quickly. US Army Lt. Henry Allen's journal of his 1885 Alaska explorations includes a drawing of an elevated log-cabin cache built by Ahtna Athabascans along the Copper River. Also, photos from turn-of-the-19th-century U.S.G.S. surveys show tall caches in Native villages, including one along the Goodpaster River, a tributary of the Tanana River about 80 miles southeast of Fairbanks.

During an 1896 journey down the Yukon River, U.S.G.S. geologist Josiah Spurr's party built tall caches to protect their supplies while investigating mining areas. In Spurr's book, *Through the Yukon Gold Diggings*, he explained that the word cache (from the French cacher — to hide) was first applied to tall caches by French Canadian voyageurs, who built the structures to temporarily store supplies. The term was later extended to similar structures built by North American aboriginal peoples.

Several 1930s ethnographic studies of Alaskan Athabascan groups describe similarly-constructed tall caches in widely separated regions, from the Dena'ina of the Kenai Peninsula to the Ingalik of the lower Yukon River. These caches had walls built from thick planks split from spruce logs, with gable roofs usually covered with either spruce or birch bark.

Tall caches are typically supported by four upright spruce poles sunk into the ground, often tilting inward towards each other. Some early caches only had three legs, and occasionally, large caches were supported by six legs. The legs' inward cant lends stability to the structure and also makes it harder for animals to climb the poles. Poles are often peeled to deter climbing.

To further discourage marauders, the poles' upper portions are sometimes banded with sheet metal. (On older caches the metal bands were often manufactured from re-purposed food tins.)

In Alaska's more developed areas tall caches have been supplanted by freezers and ground-level sheds. In many localities caches exist merely as decoration. Only "off the grid" or in areas with high electricity costs do tall caches still retain their original function.

The cache in the drawing used to stand in Pioneer Park's Gold Rush Town, next to the Two-Finns cabin. Perhaps dating to when the park was constructed in 1967, the cache was torn down in about 2013, a victim of time and decay. Donny Hayes, Pioneer Park's manager, told me that the park is not averse to rebuilding the cache if funds become available. Caches were a part of the early Fairbanks landscape — maybe someday Gold Rush Town's tall cache will return.

Sources:

- Conversation with Donny Hayes, Manager of Pioneer Park
- *Ingalik Material Culture*. Cornelius Osgood. Yale University Publications. 1940
- "Story, Storage, and Symbol: Functional Cache Architecture, Cache Narratives, and Roadside Attractions." Susan W. Fair. In *Perspectives in Vernacular Architecture*, Vol. 7. 1997
- *The Ethnography of the Tanaina*. Cornelius Osgood. Yale University Publications. 1937
- *Through the Yukon Gold Diggings*. Josiah Spurr. Eastern Publishing Company. 1900

Harry Karstens cabin at Pioneer Park in the 1990s

Harry Karstens, a.k.a. the Seventymile Kid, and his Fairbanks connection

Henry Peter (Harry) Karstens, a.k.a. The Seventymile Kid, was a legendary Alaskan outdoorsman. He is remembered as co-leader of the first successful ascent of Denali and as the first superintendent of Mount McKinley National Park (now Denali National Park). However, at the age of 19 he was also part of the first wave of Klondike stampeders heading north from Seattle in the summer of 1897.

Arriving in Dawson on Nov. 1, 1897, he quickly became disillusioned with the Klondike. Finding creeks around Dawson already staked, in December he stampeded to Henderson Creek near the Stewart River. Jack London was also mining at Henderson Creek, and one of the legends about Karstens is that the main character in London's book, *Burning Daylight*, was modeled in part on Harry.

Harry soon returned to Dawson and survived most of the winter performing odd jobs around town. In early 1898 he scouted out the gold prospects on the U.S. side of the border and that spring relocated to the Seventymile River, downriver from the new town of Eagle. (An old-timer in Eagle nicknamed him the "Seventymile Kid.") During that spring he helped layout the Eagle townsite.

Harry mined on the Seventymile for several years before accepting what he thought would be a temporary job as mail carrier between Eagle and Tanana Crossing during the winter of 1900-01. He ended up delivering mail around Interior Alaska for many years. It was Harry and fellow mail carrier Charley McGonagall who, in 1903, blazed the first winter trail from Gakona (on the Valdez-Eagle Trail) to Fairbanks.

According to Tom Walker's book, *The Seventymile Kid*, Harry considered carrying mail to be the toughest job he ever did. He is quoted as saying, "It changed my whole life in the north and filled me with wanderlust."

He and McGonagall participated in the short-lived Kantishna gold rush in 1905-06 and also ran a winter delivery service from Fairbanks to the diggings. After Kantishna petered out, Harry continued to deliver freight and passengers throughout the region and hired out as a guide.

One of the people Harry guided was Charles Sheldon (conservationist and "Father of Denali National Park"). In 1906 he led Sheldon on a two-month trip to the Toklat River on the north flank of Denali. Sheldon returned the next year, and Karstens accompanied him on a year-long excursion back to the Toklat.

Harry went on to participate in the first successful ascent of Denali in 1913. Although he did not have mountaineering experience, his level-headedness, wilderness survival skills and endurance made him indispensable during the expedition.

Thanks to the influence of Charles Sheldon, Harry became the first superintendent of Mt. McKinley National Park in 1921. He resigned from the Park Service in 1928, the same year that the road through the park to Kantishna was completed. Grant Pearson, a later Mt. McKinley National Park superintendent, wrote in his book about Karstens that, "Perhaps the park was getting a little too tame for 'The Kid.' It was losing its untamed-wilderness atmosphere."

After retiring, Harry settled in Fairbanks. He and his wife, Louise, bought and moved into a large home on Ninth Avenue. In 1953 they began work on a smaller cabin on the Ninth Avenue property (shown in the drawing) so they could rent out the larger house. The new cabin was completed in 1955.

The 20' by 18' 1 1/2-story cabin, which is now located at Pioneer Park across from the Pioneer Museum, is built of logs sawn flat on three sides. Harry's great grandson, Ken, told me that the second floor of the cabin was finished with surplus doors purchased from a steamship company. Unfortunately, the doors were removed later to install insulation. The shed-roofed room at the rear is a more recent addition.

Karstens died the same year the cabin was completed and is buried in Birch Hill Cemetery. Louise lived on in the cabin for many years. She died in 1974 at the Fairbanks Pioneer Home.

Sources:

- *Alaskaland Cabin Lore*. Alpha Delta Gamma. 1978
- Correspondence with Ken Karstens, Harry Karsten's great-grandson
- *The Seventymile kid: the lost legacy of Harry Karstens and the first ascent of Mount McKinley*. Tom Walker. Mountaineers Books. 2013
- *The Seventy Mile Kid: wilderness superintendent of Mount McKinley National Park*. Grant Pearson. Signal Press. 1957

Building 23 (Eva's Place) at Pioneer Park as it looked in 1989

"Eva's Place" can still be found at Pioneer Park

One of the oldest buildings at Pioneer Park (formerly Alaskaland) is associated with Eva McGown, who was known as Fairbanks' "official" hostess. Building 23 is a cabin located across from the Riverboat Nenana in Gold Rush Town.

According to park records this 14' by 18' log cabin was constructed in about 1903-04 on Fifth Avenue between Noble and Dunkel Street, and was used by the Orr Stage Lines as a bunkhouse. Ed Orr opened the stage line in 1904 and ran passengers and freight between Fairbanks and Valdez.

A close look at the cabin's front façade shows that the building may have served another purpose before becoming a bunkhouse. The space between the front window and door is framed in and sheathed with wooden shiplap siding, as is the wall below the window. Sans window and door, the front entry for the building was wide enough to admit a wagon or sledge, and the building may have been used by the stage line for equipment storage. Sourdough Roadhouse has a cabin (originally used for wagon storage) that shows similar modifications.

The stage line closed down in 1914. At that point Building 23's history fades into obscurity until it was donated to Alaskaland by the Nordale family.

Whatever uses the building saw during those mystery years, about the same time the stage-line closed, a tiny leprechaun of a lady arrived in Fairbanks who would figure into a later chapter of the Orr Stage Line building.

Eva Montgomery was a 31-year-old mail-order bride from Ireland. She journeyed to Fairbanks to marry Arthur McGown, part-owner of the Model Cafe on Second Avenue in downtown Fairbanks.

Eva made the monumental journey from Ireland to Alaska during the winter of 1913-14, first on a steamer from Belfast to New York, then by train across the U.S. to Seattle.

In Seattle she boarded another steamer that sailed up the Inside Passage to Valdez. From Valdez she ventured over the Valdez-Fairbanks Trail – part way by horse-drawn sledge and part way by dog sled. Eva arrived in Fairbanks on Feb. 26th and was married to Arthur that evening.

According to Jo Anne Wold's book, *The Way it Was*, Arthur and Eva lived in a small house on Perry Street. Five years into their marriage Arthur became ill and was an invalid until his death in 1930 from bone cancer.

After Arthur's death Eva found herself alone and struggling financially. She paid the bills selling magazines and taking odd jobs, but the loneliness was almost unbearable. Eva coped by comforting other lonely women and visiting patients in hospital. She was soon involved in most aspects of Fairbanks social life, and developed a keen knowledge of the housing situation in town.

Dermot Cole wrote in his book, *Fairbanks, A Gold Rush Town that beat the Odds*, that her "friendly and outgoing manner soon evolved into a one-woman housing and greeting service that became vital during the many years when demand for housing outstripped supply."

The community recognized her value and during World War II (when the military commandeered local hotels) the Fairbanks Chamber of Commerce hired her at $75 per month to run a housing office to find temporary quarters for the hundreds of people flooding into town.

She was later hired by the city (at $110 per month) and continued her social ministry from the lobby of the Nordale Hotel, where she had moved. In a 1991 interview, Joe Vogler said, "She sort of held court there … She was the town hostess, and Eva McGown was a queen in her own right."

When Alaskaland opened in 1967, Eva spent her summers there, running her hospitality center out of Building 23. She continued holding court, either at her Alaskaland cabin, or her room at the Nordale Hotel, until her death in 1972.

Sources:

- *A Gold Rush Town that Beat the Odds*. Dermot Cole. Epicenter Press. 2003
- Alaskaland Cabin Lore. Alpha Delta Gamma. 1978
- "Alaskan memories: A Fairbanks woman with a big heart of gold," In *Fearless Men and Fabulous Women: A Reporter's Memoir from Alaska & the Yukon*. Stanton Patty. Epicenter Press. 2004
- Pioneer Park property records
- *The Way it Was, Of People, Places and Things in Pioneer Interior Alaska*. Jo Anne Wold. Alaska Northwest Publishing. 1988

The "Ike" Loomis cabin at Pioneer Park as it looks today

Loomis Armored Car Service had roots in Alaska Gold Rush

According to Pioneer Park records, cabin No. 4 in Gold Rush Town is the oldest building in Fairbanks. It was constructed in summer 1903 when Fairbanks was still a raw scar in the wilderness.

E.T. Barnette had established his trading post along the Chena River in 1901 and small amounts of gold were discovered in nearby creeks in 1902. However, 1903 was the year several large gold discoveries turned the camp into a bona fide boomtown.

Judge James Wickersham visited Fairbanks in April 1903 and described the "new metropolis of the Tanana River" as a tiny, rough settlement.

According to his book, *Old Yukon: Tales, Trails and Trials*, at that time the community consisted of Barnette's trading post, a half-finished two-story log hotel, two log-cabin saloons, a half-dozen smaller residential cabins and numerous tents.

Fairbanks mushroomed that summer. Lee "Ike" Loomis, who later established Loomis Armored Car Service, was one of the many stampeders building cabins.

Six years previously, he and his wife, Jennie, were operating a feed store in Seattle. Ron Inouye wrote in a 2000 *Fairbanks Daily News-Miner* article that when news of the Klondike gold strike reached Seattle in 1897, Ike quickly joined the throngs headed north.

Landing at Dyea, he earned money packing supplies over the mountains for other gold seekers. After the White Pass and Yukon Railroad was completed, he and two brothers-in-law freighted livestock and supplies over the railroad to start a store in Dawson City.

Loomis later opened a business in Nome, but moved on to Fairbanks in 1903. Ike's wife joined him there, and he built the family a home.

With the help of his brothers-in-law, he cut his own logs and erected the 17'-wide by 21'-long, 1 1/2-story cabin, shown in the drawing. The logs were free, but metal roofing, spikes and windows for the cabin cost $800 — the equivalent of $21,000 today.

Later that year, he and his brothers-in-law took over a Fairbanks store, buying supplies from gold seekers quitting the country and reselling those supplies to new arrivals. In 1905, they opened the Cleary Creek Commercial Company (the 4Cs) at Cleary City, about 25 miles northeast of Fairbanks, and began freighting between the mining camps in the area.

Supposedly, while Ike was transporting gold between mining camps he contemplated ways to more securely transport valuable cargo. Fortunately, while pursued by the thought of being robbed out on the trail, he never experienced a theft.

His wife died during the 1918 influenza outbreak in Fairbanks, and in 1922 he became manager of the Northern Commercial Company stores at Takotna and McGrath, on the Kuskokwim River. He left Alaska for good in 1925, settling in Portland. That same year he established Loomis Armored Car Service.

When Loomis left Fairbanks, Louis Golden purchased his store and house. Pioneer Park records indicate that the leaded windows on the front of the house probably date from Golden's ownership.

Golden operated his store for many years and then sold it and the house to Paul Palfry.

Palfry converted the store, which was located at First Avenue and Wickersham Street, into a sheet-metal shop, and moved the house to a lot behind the store. There the house and store remained until relocated to Pioneer Park (then called A-67) in 1967. The cabin's lower courses of logs were damaged during Fairbanks' 1967 flood.

Those lower courses were eliminated when the cabin was reconstructed at Pioneer Park, reducing the cabin's height by several feet. The first-story doors were raised and, unfortunately, the second-story floor had to be torn out. The logs supporting the second-story floor were cut off at the cabin's outside walls, leaving only the embedded log ends.

Sources:

- *Alaskaland Cabin Lore*. Alpha Delta Gamma. 1978
- *Old Yukon: Tales, Trails and Trials*. James Wickersham. Washington Law Book Company. 1938
- "Legacy of armored car began in the gold rush." Ron Inouye, In *Fairbanks Daily News-Miner*. 5-14-2000

The *Fairbanks Daily News-Miner* building as it looks today

Fairbanks Daily News-Miner traces its history back to 1903

The 1980 book, *Adventures in Alaska Journalism since 1903*, relates that itinerant newspaper man, George M. Hill, freighted a small press from Dawson to Fairbanks in 1903. Once in Fairbanks he established the Weekly Fairbanks News, the first newspaper in town.

In 1904 he sold the paper to R.J. McChesney. Over the next two years McChesney expanded publication to semi-weekly and then daily (except Sunday).

Fairbanks was a boom town, and by 1906 there were five competing newspapers. E.T. Barnette bought the paper, then called the Fairbanks Daily News, that year, just in time for the Great 1906 fire to destroy his printing press (as well as most of downtown Fairbanks).

Serendipitously, another newspaper man, William Fentress Thompson (also lately of Dawson), arrived in town with a new press, planning to set up his own paper. Thompson's friends called him Bill, his co-workers WF. Those on the receiving end of his editorials sometimes called him "Wrong Font," a play on the editor's mark "WF," which means that a word is in the wrong size or font.

Barnette, rather than having a new press freighted in, merged his business with Thompson's. As part of the merger, Thompson was allowed to publish his morning *Tanana Daily Miner* — while the *Fairbanks Daily News* was published in the afternoon. Unfortunately, Barnette and Thompson were soon at odds and Thompson left the operation, thereafter printing his *Tanana Miner* at Chena. Barnette, meanwhile, became embroiled in legal disputes and sold the newspaper in 1908.

Thompson prospered, and purchased the *Daily News* in 1909, renaming it the *Fairbanks Daily News-Miner* — a portmanteau of the names of the *Daily News* and Thompson's previous newspaper, the *Tanana Miner*. Thompson edited the paper for the next 17 years. Along the way he absorbed competing papers and ended up publishing the only newspaper in town.

Thompson died in 1926, and three years later his widow sold the paper to Alaska industrialist Austin E. Lathrop. He built the Lathrop Building in downtown Fairbanks in 1937 and moved News-Miner operations into the basement.

The Daily News played second fiddle to Lathrop's KFAR radio station, which occupied the Lathrop Building's top floor. By the 1940s the newspaper was losing money, and Lathrop brought in Charles Willis Snedden, a newspaper efficiency expert, to diagnose the paper's problems.

In July 1950 Snedden gave Lathrop his recommendations, which included $100,000 in improvements and upgrades to the facility.

Lathrop balked at the estimated cost, and Snedden counter-offered with a proposal to buy the paper. Lathrop agreed to sell the paper to Snedden. A week later Lathrop was killed in an accident. According to Terrence Cole's book, *Fighting for the Forty-Ninth Star: C.W. Snedden and the Crusade for Alaska Statehood,* Snedden feared Lathrop's death ended the deal, but Lathrop's company, strapped for cash, went through with the sale.

Over the next few decades, Snedden gradually upgraded the News-Miner's publishing operation. In 1953, he built a two-story building adjacent to the Lathrop Building to house a rotary printing press, allowing the paper to print in full-color.

In 1965 a large one-story building was erected across the Chena River (at the paper's present location) to house all the newspaper's operations. In the early 1970s a second story was added. The building as it is now configured (shown in the drawing) is finished with cast concrete panels, with elements of the "brutalist" style, which eschews decorative design and instead highlights raw, unfinished surfaces.

In 1992, three years after Snedden's death, the newspaper was sold to Dean Singleton and Richard Scudder, co-founders of the MediaNews Group newspaper chain.

In 2015 it was announced that the News-Miner was for sale. It was purchased in 2016 by the Helen E. Snedden Foundation, a Fairbanks-based nonprofit formed by the wife of the newspaper's former publisher, Charles W. Snedden. This returned the paper to local ownership, and the foundation continues to publish the oldest continuously operating daily in Alaska.

Sources:

- "100 Years." In *Fairbanks Daily News-Miner*. 9-19-2003
- *Adventures in Alaska Journalism since 1903*. Paul Solka, Jr. & Art Bremer. Commercial Printing. 1980
- "Fairbanks Daily News-Miner sold to Snedden Foundation." Rod Boyce. In *Fairbanks Daily News-Miner*. 12-21-2015
- *Fighting for the Forty-Ninth Star: C.W. Snedden and the Crusade for Alaska Statehood*. Terrence Cole. University of Alaska Foundation. 2010

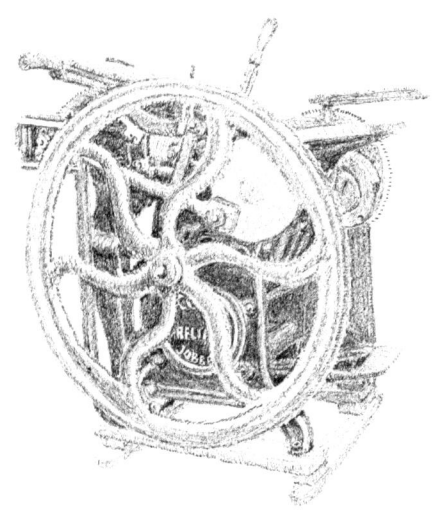

Fairbanks - North Cushman Street

St. Joseph's Hospital in the 1960s.

St. Joseph's Hospital served Fairbanks' medical needs for over 50 years

The Catholic Church sent Father Francis Monroe (Society of Jesus) to Alaska in 1894. He spent several years at missions along the Lower Yukon River before moving to the Upper Yukon after the Klondike Gold Rush began.

According to Stella Muckenthaler's 1967 master's thesis, in 1899 he was sent to the nascent community of Eagle where he established a church and St. Francis Xavier Hospital. (Fort Egbert's hospital did not accept civilian patients at that time.) As the Klondike Gold Rush died down and miners began leaving Eagle for more lucrative gold diggings, Eagle's Catholic population plummeted. That, along with the military hospital's decision to accept civilian patients, prompted Father Monroe to cast around for a new ministry location.

At the direction of his superiors, he closed St. Xavier's in 1903 and in 1904 moved to Fairbanks, intending to open a church and hospital on Garden Island, across the Chena River from Fairbanks proper. However, land prices there were high.

For a time he turned his attention to church building, but at the urging of local residents he again began planning for a hospital. With financial backing from Fairbanks residents and businesses, he purchased Garden Island property on May 19, 1906.

Three days later a fire razed much of the Fairbanks downtown, and many business owners were forced to withdraw their pledges. Only a loan from Father Joseph Crimont, Apostolic Prefect for Alaska, allowed work on the hospital to proceed.

The 1906 hospital was a 42' by 76' wood-frame three-story structure with a flat roof. Patient's rooms and medical facilities were located on the second and third floors, while a chapel, kitchen and quarters for the sisters occupied the first floor. A full basement contained the heating plant and laundry.

Work on the building was completed by late autumn, and St. Joseph's Hospital opened on Thanksgiving Day in 1906. For several years it was operated by the Sisters of St. Anne and then by Benedictine Sisters. In 1910 the Sisters of Providence assumed responsibility for St. Joseph's, which they continued until the hospital closed in 1968.

By the 1930s the hospital needed to expand. An Oct. 28, 1935, *Daily News-Miner article* relates that a 43' by 61' wood-frame three story addition was constructed on the hospital's west end that year. The addition provided a new front entrance, more rooms for patients, up-to-date operating facilities, office space, elevator and coal-fired heating plant.

By the 1950s the hospital was forced to expand again. In 1951 a 43' by 120' three-story poured-concrete addition was built on the north end of the 1935 addition, almost doubling the hospital's footprint. The drawing shows this iteration of St. Joseph's.

According to a 1956 Sisters of Providence brochure, the 1951 addition, which paralleled what was then North Cushman Street, housed new diagnostic and testing facilities, store rooms, a dietary department, additional patient rooms and a new power plant.

In the years following the new addition's completion, the second and third floors of the original hospital were torn down. The first floor, housing the chapel and sister's residential quarters remained in use.

The August 1967 Fairbanks flood forced the evacuation of St. Joseph's and damaged the facility. The Sisters of Providence announced that the order did not have the resources to repair or expand, and the hospital closed in June 1968. The Fairbanks community immediately began planning for a new community hospital, and Fairbanks Memorial Hospital opened in 1972.

St. Joseph's was sold to the city and the wood-frame sections were torn down. The 1952 poured-concrete addition stood derelict for many years, until it was renovated and expanded to become Denali State Bank.

Sources:

- Alaska mission collection, 1887-1955. Society of Jesuits, Oregon Province. At UAF Rasmussen Library
- *Fairbanks Daily News-Miner* articles. October 28, 1935, November 13, 1952
- Interpretive display in lobby of Denali State Bank
- Sisters of Providence photo archives. Providence Archives website. Seattle, Washington
- "The inception and early developmental years of St. Joseph Hospital, Fairbanks, Alaska." Stella Muckenthaler. Catholic University of America – Master's thesis. 1967
- William Stegemeyer Photo Collection. University of Alaska Archives

Railroad Industrial Area - Phillips Field Road

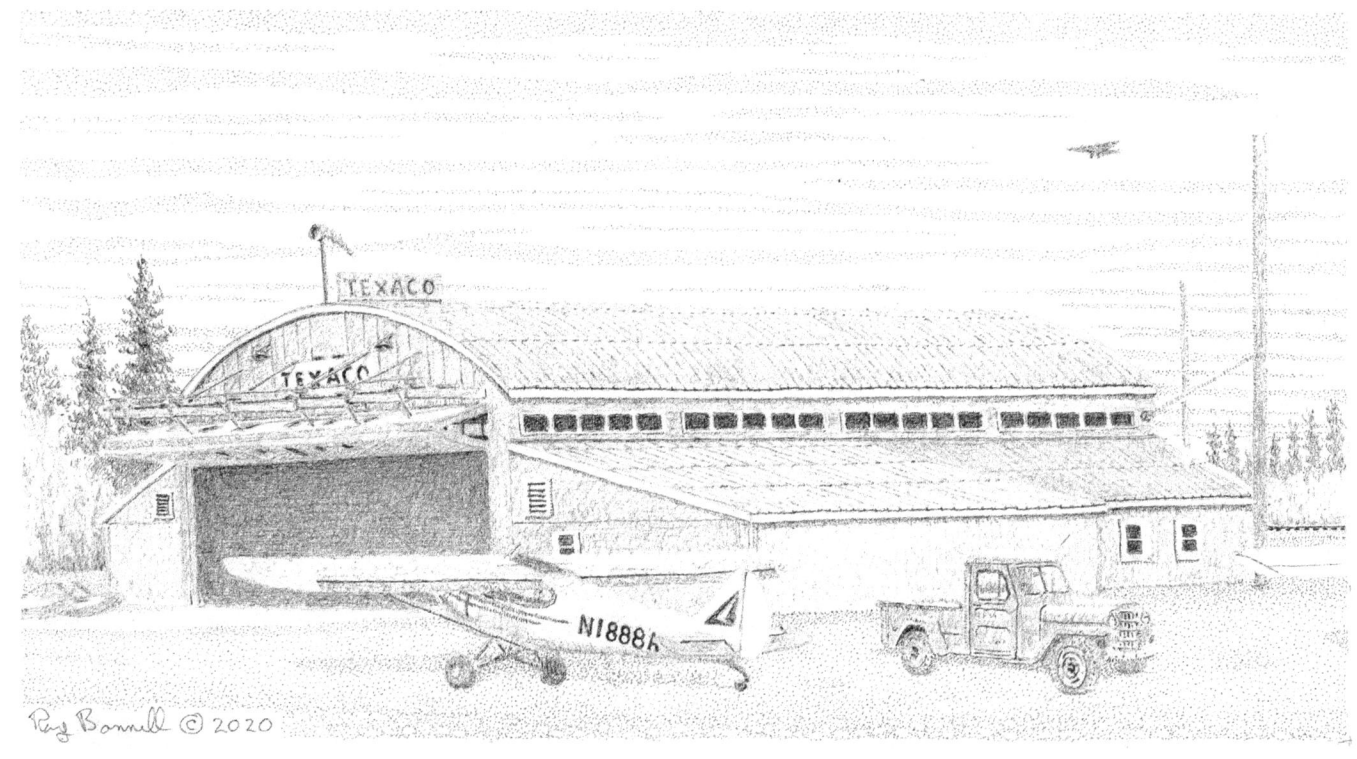

The Bachner Air Services hangar at Phillips Field in the 1950s

Phillips Field served Fairbanks aviation community's needs for 40 years

During Fairbanks' post-World War II population boom, development pressure forced the relocation of the community's airport, Weeks Field. The airport, less than a mile from downtown, moved eight miles farther away, to its present location at Fairbanks International Airport.

In a 2013 talk given by Andy Bachner, son of one of the founders of Phillips Field, he related that many operators at Weeks Field could not afford the move to the new airport. Some individuals were also leery of regulations and oversight that a government-funded airport might impose.

A group of Weeks Field operators coalesced to discuss establishing a "pilot-oriented" airfield offering services such as maintenance and fueling; and catering to private pilots, air-taxi operators, guides, and other small operators.

They wanted an airport close to town which could serve wheeled, ski- and float-equipped planes, and that minimized costs for pilots.

Most were also independent-minded and valued their privacy. Bachner related that "Air taxi guys were kind of like miners. Supposedly nobody ever made a profit, but you didn't want the other guy ever seeing how much business you were doing." Their opposition to government oversight also meant they wanted a privately-funded and run airport.

The group eventually whittled itself down to four: Jesse Bachner, Dave Phillips, Howley Evans, and Gordon Mitchell; who set about finding suitable land. They were contacted by Carroll Phillips, who had a 150-acre homestead on the north side of the Chena River, beyond the Alaska Railroad (ARR) yards, and between the river and Noyes Slough.

Being a civic-minded person, Carroll was willing to lease (for a minimal amount) the part of his homestead south of the ARR tracks to a partnership formed by Bachner, Phillips, Evans and Mitchell. That partnership, Phillips Field Inc. (named for Carroll Phillips) agreed to pay taxes and liability insurance, plus make all improvements.

The partners (and their families) performed much of the work developing and operating the airport themselves, with volunteer help from area pilots. Work began on Phillips Field in April 1950 and a dirt strip was completed that summer.

The runway was gradually improved, and eventually was 3,600' long, with 1,000' paved and 2,600' graveled. The hangar shown in the drawing, the airfield's maintenance facility, was built a year after the initial airstrip was completed.

Until the late 1970s, most air taxis operators, guides, and other small-plane pilots in the Fairbanks area were based at Phillips Field. However, by the 1970s, city, borough and state transportation planners believed a new ground transportation corridor was needed on the north side of the Chena river. Planners studied the issue for several years and finally decided the most economical route would run down the center of the Phillips Field runway. In 1977 it was announced that Phillips Field would close within a few years.

Protests and budget constraints delayed the closing for 14 years. However, knowing that the airport would eventually close, aviation businesses and private pilots began moving to other locations. Metro Field, Chena Marina, North Pole Airport, Lakloey Air Park, and several smaller strips were developed due to Phillips Field's impending closure. A 1976 aerial photo of Phillips Field shows more than 100 aircraft parked there. A 1986 photo shows about 30, and by 1990 only about a dozen aircraft remained.

Phillips Field officially closed on Sept. 1, 1991, but a few flights occurred after that. Chuck Gray, one of the most ardent protesters against closing the field, told me that he flew his Piper Apache off the runway on May 31, 1992. A week later — the runway already torn up — he flew his Piper Super Cub off a hastily-graded access road, the last flight from Phillips Field. That is Chuck's Piper sitting in front of the hangar in the drawing.

Sources:

- "Andy Bachner speaks at the Aviation Museum, Pioneer Park in Fairbanks, Alaska on October 15, 2013." Andy Bachner. UAF Oral History collection.
- Conversation with Chuck Gray, long-time Fairbanks resident and pilot. 2020
- "Jess Bachner is interviewed on January 12, 1985 by William Schneider at Phillips Field." Jess Bachner. UAF Oral History collection
- "Phillips Field." From *Abandoned and Little-know Airfields: Alaska* website, <http://airfields-freeman.com/AK/Airfields_AK.htm#phillips> 2020.
- Pioneer Air Museum display about Phillips Field.

Fairbanks - College Road, Fountainhead Antique Auto Museum

Wheelmen pedaled winter trails during Yukon and Alaska gold rushes

Many people view winter biking as a recent phenomenon. However, bicycles came north with gold-seekers over 100 years ago. The 1897/98 Klondike Gold Rush occurred near the peak of a world-wide bicycle craze in the 1890s, and it was only natural for some stampeders to bring their bicycles with them.

Terrence Cole's book, *Wheels on Ice, Bicycling in Alaska 1898-1908*, presents first-hand accounts from several gold rush-era bicyclists. It tells of a Seattle newspaper which wrote in March 1900 that, "scarcely a steamer leaves for the North that does not carry bicycles," and of the *Skagway Daily Alaska* newspaper, which reported that in the spring of 1901 about 250 bicycles were on the trail to Dawson City. Photos in the University of Alaska archives also show bicyclists queued up behind horse-drawn sleds and dogteams climbing over Thompson Pass along the Valdez-Fairbanks Trail.

Bicycles, or "wheels" as they were called, made some sense as winter transportation for economy-minded prospectors. Bikes of that era had simple but strong frames made of tu-

Gold rush-era wheelman. From 1903 photograph

bular steel. They had one fixed-gear, few complicated parts, and tires could be easily repaired. Priced at $35 to $100, they were less expensive to own and operate that a team of huskies. Bicyclists also never had to go outside at 40 degrees below zero to feed their iron steeds.

The wheels glided within the 2" track left by a sled runner, and bicyclists (called "wheelmen") could outpace most others on the trail. Utilizing roadhouses to provide food and a warm place to sleep, minimally equipped wheelmen could travel most of the region's main trails, at least when the terrain and weather permitted.

While bicycles ran well on packed trails, pedaling through unpacked snow or during a snow storm was almost impossible. Bicycles also didn't fare well in heavy winds.

John Clark, in a description of his 1906 bicycle ride from Valdez to Fairbanks, wrote of battling winds along the Delta River. Of another wheelman headed in the opposite direction against the wind Clark reported, "He struggled manfully for about ten minutes and made about 50 feet backwards. He then laid the wheel down on the ice, untied a small sack under the saddle and put the package in his pocket. He took up the wheel, carried it to a pile of rocks…, lifted it as high as he could above his head and then slammed it down on the rocks and started up stream on foot. "

Bicycles also had to be walked or carried up steep grades. They were prone to breakdowns (often far from the nearest habitation). Bearings froze, and pedals or handlebars sometimes snapped off in a fall. Injuries caused by accidents, snowblindness (from the eyestrain of following narrow sled tracks) and frostbite were also constant dangers. Their compatriots often viewed wheelmen as being slightly addled.

Perhaps the most travelled bicycle route was the 400-mile winter trail between Whitehorse and Dawson City. The drawing is based on a 1903 photograph of an unnamed wheelman who raced over the trail in a record-setting five days. The gent was evidently a dedicated racer. He even had toe-clips on his pedals.

From the chainwheel design and other details it appears his bicycle may be a Pierce Arrow. A similar 1897 Ivers & Johnson bicycle can be seen at Fountainhead Antique Auto Museum here in Fairbanks.

A few of the hardiest wheelmen pedaled the 1200 miles from Dawson City to the Seward Peninsula in early 1900 to join the Nome Stampede. Ed Jesson and Max Hirschberg were two of those adventurers.

Hirschberg wrote of breaking his bicycle's chain just east of Nome. With a stiff wind at his back, he scavenged a stick from beside the trail, stuffed it inside the back of his coat and sailed the rest of the way.

Jesson had fewer difficulties navigating the route, and he completed the Dawson-to-Nome trip in 36 days. According to a 2004 *Alaska Magazine* article, winter bike trekkers Andy Sterns (from Fairbanks), and Frank Wolf and Kevin Vallely (from Vancouver B.C.) pedaled a similar route in 2003, taking 40 days to reach Nome. I guess newer isn't always faster.

Sources:

- *Hard Drive to the Klondike, Historic Resource Study for Klondike Gold Rush National Historical Park, Chapter 3*. National Park Service. 1998
- Photo of bicyclist on Valdez-Fairbanks Trail from Falcon Joslin papers, University of Alaska Fairbanks Archives
- Photo of Whitehorse-to-Dawson bicyclist from Selid-Bassoc collection, University of Alaska Fairbanks Archives
- "Rollin' on the River: adventurers pedal down the Yukon River on a route first bicycled 104 years ago." Andy Sterns. In *Alaska Magazine*. Vol. 7. No. 3, April 2004
- *Wheels on Ice, Bicycling in Alaska 1898-1908*. Edited by Terrence Cole. Alaska Northwest Publishing. 1985

Quonset huts were common in Fairbanks after the end of World War II. This Quonset hut, in Lemeta, is one of the few remaining.

Government surplus helped build Alaska

Since before statehood, government surplus has been instrumental in the development of Eastern Interior Alaska. The evidence of its importance, while disappearing, can still be occasionally seen across the region.

For almost four decades after the U.S. purchased Russia's interests in Alaska in 1867, the area was essentially ignored by the federal government. Not until the Klondike gold rush in neighboring Canada did the U.S. begin investing resources and men in developing the region.

In the late 1890s and early 1900s, the U.S. Army built six posts in Alaska: at Nome, St. Michael, Tanana, Eagle, Valdez and Haines. It also constructed the Washington-Alaska Military Cable and Telegraph System (WAMCATS) to link the posts with each other and with the rest of the United States. All the forts except Fort Seward at Haines were closed by the 1920s. When they closed, many of their buildings were converted to other uses or torn down for building materials and firewood. For instance, of the 45 buildings originally at Fort Egbert at Eagle, only five remain today.

However, even before the posts closed, residents were making use of surplus government materials. WAMCATS landlines began to be replaced with wireless telegraphy within a few years of the line's completion, and sections of the line were systematically shut down. The first to close was the line from Eagle to Gulkana, closed by 1911. Telegraph stations along that segment were abandoned.

Local residents scavenged what they could from many of the abandoned stations. One of the items recycled was corrugated metal roofing. The 1976 BLM report, *They Didn't Come in Four-Wheel Drives: An Introduction to Fortymile History*, relates that the reason some cabins in the area were in such good condition was that their sod roofs had been replaced with abandoned government roofing.

World War II brought a new influx of federal personnel and resources into the Territory. With the end of the war, a surplus of materials, vehicles and structures became available for the general population to use. Many a pair of Army-surplus snowshoes grace the walls of homesteads across the state.

Government surplus trucks found their way into civilian ownership throughout Southcentral and Eastern Interior Alaska. Many swamp buggies used for hunting, including the one owned by my wife's father, began as military trucks. The remains of cast-aside government surplus vehicles can still be found scattered across the countryside.

Civilians also acquired surplus World War II buildings, much appreciated with the acute housing shortage in both Fairbanks and Anchorage after the war. According to the Army publication, *World War II heritage of Ladd Field*, about 100 buildings were erected at Ladd Field (now Fort Wainwright) during World War II, most of them temporary units. After the war, most of the temporary buildings were torn down, but some were converted to civilian use. The old Tamarac Inn on Minnie Street was cobbled together from several surplus Ladd Field structures.

The Quonset hut shown in the drawing, located in Lemeta (a 1950s-era Fairbanks subdivision), is probably from Ladd Field. Quonset huts derive their name from Quonset Point in Rhode Island, where the structures were first manufactured. With their distinctive curved side-walls and roofs, Quonset huts were once common sights — used as houses, garages, shops, warehouses, even stores and restaurants.

Quonset huts have steel ribs and curved metal sheathing, but other similarly-designed structures erected at Ladd Field utilized different materials. Pacific huts used plywood ribs and sheathing, while Jamesway huts were constructed of plywood ribbing covered by insulated fabric.

All found their way into civilian usage after the war, but Quonset huts, because of their metal construction are the only survivors. Even they are gradually disappearing, victims of suburban sprawl and urban redevelopment.

Sources:

- *Buildings of Alaska*. Alison K. Hoagland. Oxford University Press. 1993
- Fairbanks North Star Borough property records
- *They didn't come in Four-Wheel Drives, An Introduction to Fortymile History*. Terry Haynes. Bureau of Land Management. 1976
- *The World War II Heritage of Ladd Field*. Cathy Price. Center for Environmental Management of Military Lands. 2004

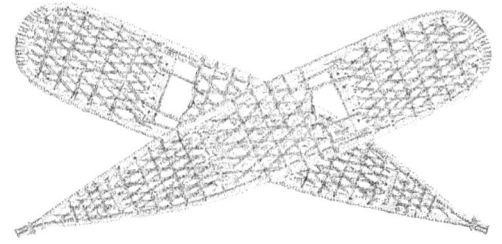

University of Alaska, Fairbanks, Tanana Loop

Elmer Rasmuson Library at the University of Alaska - Fairbanks campus

Rasmuson Library carries on the dream of Charles Bunnell

The library at the University of Alaska, Fairbanks had an inauspicious beginning. According to Ted Ryberg (the university's librarian in 1970), while the university's predecessor, the Alaska Agricultural College and School of Mines, began classes on Sept. 18, 1922, the college library had a slower start, not accessioning its first book until 10 days later.

The college was perennially short of funds. However, through the determination of its first president, Charles Bunnell, its library amassed over 2,000 volumes during the college's first year. Bunnell's long-term goal had been to acquire "everything ... published on Alaska by Alaskans." That goal has been amply met in the university's modern, Rasmuson Library, which is one of largest libraries in Alaska, and one of the state's premier research libraries.

From 1922 until 1935 the library was housed in Old Main building, which stood where the Bunnell Building is now. In 1935 the library moved to the newly-finished second floor of the college gymnasium (now Signer's Hall). By 1960, when it moved to the newly-constructed Bunnell Building, the library housed slightly more than 70,000 volumes.

In all its locations, the library was pressed for space, and discussions about building a new facility began soon after the library moved into the Bunnell Building. Planning for a new library began in 1961, and a new facility might have been built sooner had state funding not been consumed in dealing with the aftermath of the 1964 Good Friday Earthquake.

Funding was finally approved in 1966, and except for disruptions caused by the 1967 Chena River flood, construction proceeded until the Rasmuson Library was completed in 1970. The library is named in honor of Elmer E. Rasmuson, ardent university supporter and former President of the Board of Regents.

Francis Bernardo Mayer, an Anchorage architect, designed the library, as well as the adjacent fine-arts complex. Mayer was responsible for designing many Alaskan public buildings during the mid-20th century, including Gould and Grant Hall at Alaska Methodist University, the Anchorage International Airport North Terminal, and UAF's Bunnell Building.

The library and fine arts complex were designed in the International Style. The structures are built of poured concrete, with a pebble-dash exterior finish (pebbles sprayed on and pressed into the still-wet concrete). They have flat roofs with wide cantilevered eaves that appear to float over the arched window-bays located just below the cornice.

At the time of the library's 1970 opening, the six-story 113,156-square-foot building housed almost 220,000 volumes, with the capacity to house 400,000 volumes. However, within a decade the facility contained over 740,000 volumes, forcing the university to add 68,616 square-feet of space in 1985. The new expansion allowed the library to establish the Alaska and Polar Regions Collections and Archives department. The facility received additional renovations and modifications in 2001.

With the expansion of its holdings to include more than just books, the library states that it now houses over 1.2 million items. In addition to its general collections, the library houses special collections including microforms; government documents; manuscripts and historic photographs; the Alaska Film Archives, containing Alaska-related films and video; the Alaska Native Languages Archive, managed by the Alaska Native Languages Center; a rare book and map collection (one of the world's best collections focused on polar regions); an oral history collection; and the Alaska book and periodical collection.

In addition, the library has numerous electronic media resources including online databases, books and streaming video. A number of the library's holdings such as select historic photographs and oral history recordings are also available online (no need to visit campus) through websites such as Project Jukebox and the Alaska Digital Archives.

The library welcomes the general public, school visits, and researchers from around the world.

Sources:

- *Buildings of Alaska*. Alison K. Hoagland. Oxford University Press. 1993
- Correspondence with Karen Jensen, the Director of Libraries at the Rasmuson Library
- "Dedication of Elmer E. Rasmuson Library at the University of Alaska in Fairbanks, Alaska on May 3, 1970 with William O'Neill, Ted Ryberg, Terence Armstrong and William Wood" (sound recording). UAF Oral History collection
- Elmer E. Rasmuson Library webpage
- "Rasmuson Library, UAF." From *UA Journey* webpage

A Yukon River fishwheel circa 1950. Based on historic photograph.

Interior Alaska's once numerous fishwheels dwindle in number

It may surprise people that the picturesque fishwheels that are so much a part of Interior Alaska life, and so often associated with Athabascan Indian culture, are not indigenous to Alaska or Canada. Athabascans customarily used weirs, nets and traps for fishing, but adopted fishwheels when the new technology was introduced at the end of the 19th century.

Their origins are unknown, but fishwheels have been used for centuries throughout the world, including in China, Japan, Europe, Scandinavia and the United States. Fishwheels in the U.S. date to 1829, when they were used to harvest shad from North Carolina rivers. Their usage soon spread to nearby states.

In 1879 fishwheels were introduced to the Columbia River, where they gained favor in intercepting migrating salmon. By 1905 over seventy-five commercial fishwheels operated along the Columbia, harvesting enormous quantities of fish. According to a 2005 article in *Subsistence*

Management Information newsletter, in 1913 one Columbia River wheel captured 70,000 pounds of salmon in a single day. Systematic over-harvesting of Columbia River salmon led Oregon to ban fishwheels in 1926, and Washington to follow suit in 1935.

Canneries may have introduced fishwheels to Southeast Alaska. I found a 1908 photo from the University of Washington archives showing an industrial-looking Taku River fishwheel with a basket at least 20' wide, undoubtedly used commercially.

However, it was goldseekers and their followers who brought fishwheels to Interior Alaska and the Yukon during the Klondike gold rush. In the late 1890s and early 1900s fishwheels sprang up along the Yukon River from about Anvik on the Middle Yukon, upstream into Canada. Fishwheel usage eventually spread to other river systems, including the Copper, Kuskokwim and Skwentna Rivers.

Athabascans and Westerners both used fishwheels, and in 1918 there were 393 fishwheels operating along the Yukon and its tributaries. The *Subsistence Management* article states that fishwheels were ineffective on the Lower Yukon with its meandering waters. Hudson Stuck, in his book, V*oyages on the Yukon and its Tributaries*, states that with the Lower Yukon's abundant salmon runs, traditional methods of catching salmon were more than adequate and fishwheels unnecessary.

The drawing, which shows a fishwheel with rounded-end basket (common on the Yukon River) is based on a historic photo taken in about 1950 near Fort Yukon. The publication, F*ishwheels and How to Build Them*, states that while modern fishwheels often incorporate naturally-occurring and store-bought materials, fishwheels can be built entirely of birch or spruce logs, poles and wooden pegs. It appears that the only store-bought materials used in the drawing's fishwheel were the wire mesh for the basket, and possibly the milled lumber for the fish catch-box and paddles. Older photos depict wheels with even the catch-boxes constructed of cribbed logs.

Another common variation of the fishwheel uses squared-end baskets. The book, *Alaskan's How To Handbook*, quotes expert fishwheel builder and long-time Interior resident, Bill Taylor, as saying that square-ended fishwheel baskets, with their sturdier basket frames, are stronger than rounded-end baskets, and more suitable to debris-laden rivers such as the Tanana.

Once, fishwheels were common even on the Chena River. I have an acquaintance who remembers, as a child, watching fishwheels just downstream from the Cushman Street bridge.

The number of operational fishwheels throughout Alaska has declined over the years. In rural Alaska, snow machines have replaced dog teams (prodigious fish consumers), and declining salmon runs in recent years have contributed significantly to the reduced number of fishwheels.

According to the Alaska Department of Fish and Game, only 69 fishwheels operated along the Alaska section of Yukon River and its tributaries in 2015. Fishwheels on the Chena River are now just a memory, but display models can be seen around town, such as the one outside the University's Harper Building on Geist Road.

Sources:

- *Alaskan's How To Handbook*. John Dart. Interior Trapper's Association. 1981
- *Arctic-Yukon-Kuskokwim Area Salmon Fishing History*. Steven Pennoyer, Kenneth Middleton & Melvan Morris. State of Alaska Department of Fish and Game. 1998
- *Fishwheels and How to Build Them*. Adult Literacy Laboratory. Anchorage Community College. 1979
- Photo of Yukon River fishwheel taken by Frank Whaley. In the Wien Collection at the Anchorage Museum
- "Wheels spin into 2nd century in Alaska." In *Subsistence Management Information* newsletter. Vol. 5, No. 1, March 2005

Old Chena townsite building as it was being prepped for the return trip to Chena

110-year-old building returns home to Chena

In early 1901, several months before E.T. Barnette's party landed on a bank several miles up the Chena River, George Belt and Nathan Hendricks opened a trading post on the south bank of the Tanana River, across from the Chena River's mouth.

During the next year prospecting in the hills north of the Tanana increased, and the Washington-Alaska Military Cable and Telegraph System (WAMCATS) began re-routing a portion of its telegraph line along the north bank of the Tanana River. Consequently, Belt and Hendricks moved their trading post to the Tanana's north bank in the spring of 1902.

Buoyed by an influx of stampeders from Rampart (established in about 1897), a town sprang into existence south of the Chena's mouth. At first it was called Tanana City, then Chenoa (later shortened to Chena).

Belt and Hendricks reserved a building lot in the center of town, and others staked lots around them.

Chena's early days were a helter-skelter free-for-all. Lot jumping was common, and the only way to enforce a claimant's rights was with force. According to Terrence Cole's book, *Crooked Past—The History of a Frontier Mining Camp: Fairbanks, Alaska*, two argonauts who had staked a lot and built a cabin at Chena returned from a trip up the Chena River to find that all their possessions, including their cabin, had been stolen.

It was not until Martin Harrais arrived at Chena in the fall of 1903 that some semblance of order began to appear. Harrais was a business associate of Falcon Joslin, who was the driving force behind construction of the Tanana Mines Railway (TMR), later renamed the Tanana Valley Railroad.

Harrais came to Chena to map a preliminary route for the railway. He went on to become the first mayor of the town.

His party wagered that Chena had a better location than Fairbanks, and that Fairbanks could not survive. The railway route chosen by Harrais's party ran from Chena to the foot of Pedro Dome northeast of Fairbanks, and bypassed Fairbanks entirely. Within a year, however, it was decided to extend the line to Fairbanks.

With Chena becoming the TVR's southern terminus, the town quickly grew, for a time rivaling Fairbanks. During its boom years of 1904-1905, it boasted numerous stores and saloons, a telegraph office, at least one church, a hospital, several newspapers, police and fire departments, bustling waterfront, and large railroad yard.

Prosperity was not to last though. While Fairbanks grew, Chena shrank. By 1910 about 4,000 people lived in the Fairbanks/Garden Island/Graehl area, while less than 200 called Chena home.

In 1915 Nenana was chosen as the northern headquarters for construction of the Alaska Railroad, and the next year many of Chena's deserted buildings were disassembled and floated to Nenana. Others were moved to Fairbanks. By 1920, when the railroad tracks to Chena were torn up, Chena had only 18 residents.

The building shown in the drawing is one of the structures moved from Chena to Fairbanks. It is a wood-frame structure, about 8' by 20', with a shed roof and false front. The structure was probably built between 1904 and 1907, and the false front suggests that it was once a commercial building.

It was moved to Weeks Field (where Noel Wien Library is now), which was Fairbanks' first airport. During World War II the building was used by the Civil Aeronautics Authority as housing. When Fairbanks International Airport opened in 1951, Weeks Field closed, and the old building was relocated to the property of Alaska Stewart Linck on 10th Avenue.

Linck's son, James Moody, inherited the structure upon her death. After Moody died in 2017, his estate donated the building to the Alaska State Division of Parks and Outdoor Recreation.

The building was returned to Chena in the winter of 2018-19. Now located at Chena Pump Wayside, it is awaiting restoration.

Sources:

- Correspondence with Martin Gutoski, Fairbanks historian
- *Crooked Past—The History of a Frontier Mining Camp: Fairbanks, Alaska*. Terrence Cole. University of Alaska Press. 1991
- "City of Fairbanks impounds trailer carrying historic building." Sam Friedman. In *Fairbanks Daily News-Miner*. 11-16-2018
- Signage at Chena Pump Wayside
- *Tanana Valley Railroad: The Gold Dust Line*. Nicholas Deely. Denali Designs. 1996
- U.S. Census, 1910, 1920

Fairbanks - Murphy Dome Road

Murphy Dome radar site near Fairbanks

Peaceful Murphy Dome was once a Cold War radar surveillance site

Murphy Dome, named by prospectors in the early 1900s, is a 2,930-foot-tall mountain 20 miles northwest of Fairbanks. It is the highest point in the area, and with a summit almost 2,500 feet above the Tanana River Valley, it has a commanding view of the countryside. Easily accessible via Murphy Dome Road, it is popular with recreational users, whether berry-pickers and hikers in the summer, or aurora viewers during the winter.

However, 50 year ago, a different clientele frequented the area. Beginning in the early 1950s, Murphy Dome was the site of a major Cold War-era radar surveillance facility.

After World War II, relations between the United States and its former ally, the Soviet Union, quickly soured. In response to the Soviet military threat across the Bering Straits, Alaska became important for the strategic defense of the United States.

According to Air Force reports, as part of a comprehensive air defense system, 12 Aircraft Control and Warning (AC&W) stations were constructed across Alaska during the 1950s. One of those, the system's Northern Alaska Control Center, was built at Murphy Dome.

Construction of the Murphy Dome Air Force Station began in 1950. The facility was completed by autumn 1951, and fully operational by spring 1952. At the height of operations, the facility covered 846 acres, with four radar domes and 18 other buildings, including housing for about 140 military personnel and a handful of civilians. All buildings were connected by enclosed passage-ways. The facility was considered a remote station and there was no family housing.

The facility did have a few amenities. The station had a rec hall, as well as a softball diamond and ski area. The website "Alaska's Lost Ski Areas," states that the station had a small ski slope with a lift cobbled together using car wheels as pulleys for a rope-tow.

In addition to radar surveillance, the site also hosted telecommunications facilities. In the early years of Alaska's strategic defense system, communications between scattered remote sites were limited to high-frequency and very-high-frequency radio. Beginning in the mid 1950s the Air Force constructed a more reliable microwave telecommunications system. This system, called White Alice, linked not only AC&W sites, but eventually Distant Early Warning (DEW) Line and Ballistic Missile Early Warning System (BMEWS) sites. A White Alice station was installed at Murphy Dome in 1957.

With the advent of satellite communications, the White Alice system was gradually phased out. The Murphy Dome microwave facility was deactivated in 1979.

In the early 1980s a new regional operations control center for state-wide military radar surveillance was constructed at Elmendorf Air Force Base (now Joint Base Elmendorf-Richardson) in Anchorage. Modern satellite communications systems allowed the new center to manage all air defense operations in Alaska.

Manned remote radar sites were no longer required, so in 1983, the staffing at Murphy Dome was reduced to 10 civilian personnel.

In 1986 the Murphy Dome radar site was converted to a minimally-manned radar station (MMRS), with radar information automatically relayed to Elmendorf AFB. Only maintenance personnel are needed, and they are not required to live on-site.

In 1987, the site was cleaned up and most of the buildings were demolished and buried on-site. The only buildings that remained were two radar domes, the decommissioned White Alice site and several ancillary structures.

Now, only one radar dome and its support facilities remain. While people can roam most of Murphy Dome's summit, the still-active radar facility is in a restricted area. Take photos, but don't trespass.

Sources:

- "Alaskan Air Defenses." On *Online Air Defense Radar Museum* webpage, www.radomes.org/museum. No date
- "Final Site Investigation Report, Murphy Dome LLRS, Alaska." United States Air Force. 1993
- "Management Action Plan, Final, Murphy Dome LRRS, Alaska." United States Air Force Environmental Restoration Program. 1995
- "Murphy Dome AFS Rope Tow." On *Alaska's Lost Ski Areas Project* webpage, www.alsap.org. No date
- "Murphy Dome Air Force Station." On *Fort Wiki,* a website documenting the historic forts of Canada and the United States, www.fortwiki.com. No date

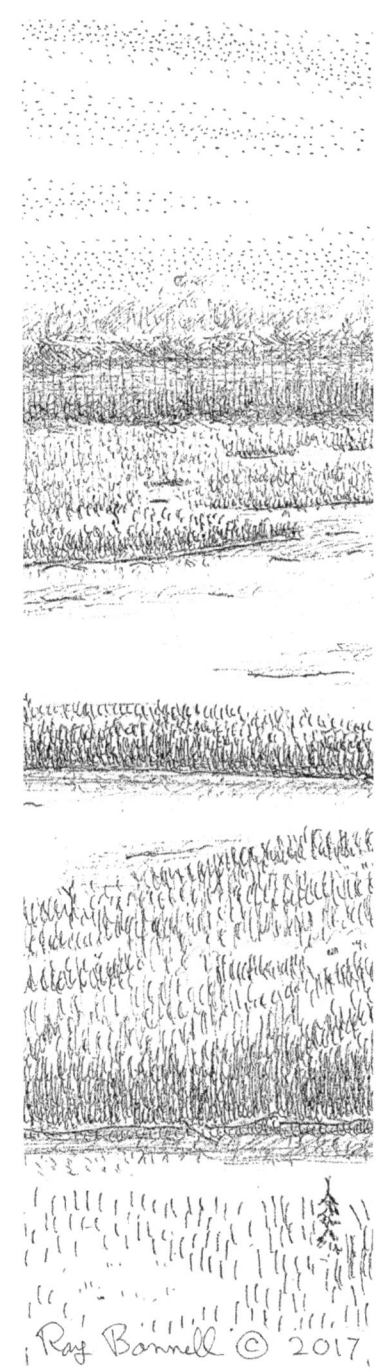

Truth be Told

by Alaskan artist, Nina Crumrine
In June 1945 issue of *Alaska Life*,
the Territorial Magazine

*If you were frank my friend,
Was it gold of sunset sky,
Rather that metal's lure,
Which called you to latitudes high?*

*Was it the autumn flame
Of golden birch in the wood
Along the silvery streams
Which you thought good?*

*Was it the vast untamed
Stretches of elbow room,
Where one might lean on the brink
Of Time to Eternity grown?*

*Did these clear, cold streams
You waded knee deep for gold
Give you riches much more
In courage and strength tenfold?*

*In silent winter watch,
With the calm Pole star for light,
Did you trade the crowd's pain
For a vision of life more bright?*

*Did those cloud-wreathed peaks above
Beckon with Nature's hand.
Saying, "Come. My son be glad—
Here is the Promised Land!"*

*Sourdough, thoughtful and gray,
Graceful in growing old,
Tell us the truth—you have found
Treasures greater than gold!*

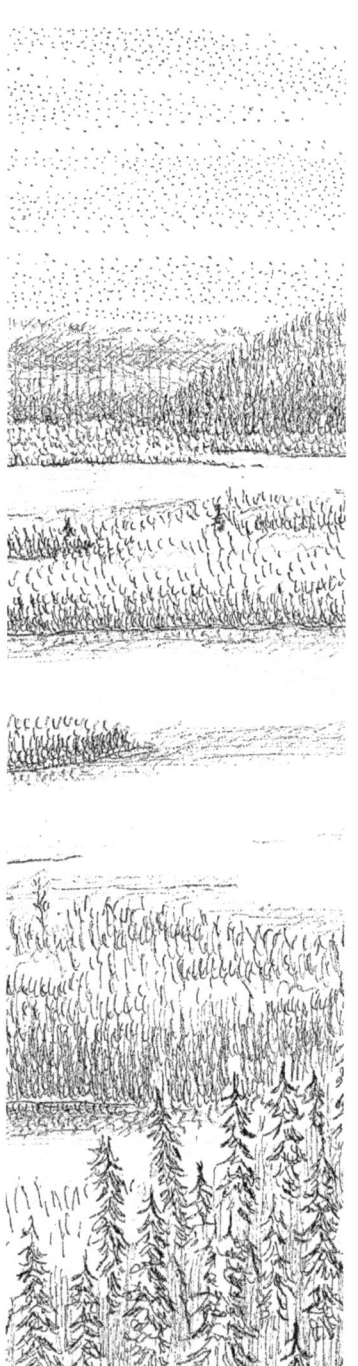

www.ingramcontent.com/pod-product-compliance
Lightning Source LLC
Chambersburg PA
CBHW081113080526
44587CB00021B/3575